P9-DFI-395

THE GOD
WHO WOULD
BE KNOWN

Also by John M. Templeton:

The Templeton Plan: 21 Steps to Personal Success and Real Happiness

THE GOD WHO WOULD BE KNOWN

Revelations of the Divine in Contemporary Science

John M. Templeton and Robert L. Herrmann

HARPER & ROW, PUBLISHERS, SAN FRANCISCO

New York, Grand Rapids, Philadelphia, St. Louis
London, Singapore, Sydney, Tokyo

Acknowledgments are on page 205.

THE GOD WHO WOULD BE KNOWN: Revelations of the Divine in Contemporary Science. Copyright © 1989 by John M. Templeton and Robert L. Herrmann. All rights reserved. Printed in the United States of America. No part of this book may be used or reproduced in any manner whatsoever without written permission except in the case of brief quotations embodied in critical articles and reviews. For information address Harper & Row, Publishers, Inc., 10 East 53rd Street, New York, NY 10022.

FIRST EDITION

Library of Congress Cataloging-in-Publication Data

Templeton, John,
   The God who would be known.

   1. Religion and science—1946-   .
2. God. I. Hermann, Robert L.
II. Title.
BL240.2.T43 1989   261.5'5   88-45988
ISBN 0-06-250867-9

89 90 91 92 93 HC 10 9 8 7 6 5 4 3 2 1

Dedicated to the pioneering research scientists
who are discovering the ongoing and accelerating
creative process and millions more creations by
the Creator.

LINCOLN CHRISTIAN COLLEGE AND SEMINARY

80433

Contents

1. The God Who Would Be Known

Men of Athens! I see that in every way you are very religious. For as I walked around and observed your objects of worship, I even found an altar with this inscription: To The Unknown God. . . .

The God who made the world and everything in it is the Lord of heaven and earth and does not live in temples built by hands. And He is not served by human hands, as if He needed anything, because He Himself gives all men life and breath and everything else.[1]

SCIENCE AND THE TRANSCENDENT

This is a book about signals of transcendence, about pointers to the Infinite that are coming to us not from mystics but instead through the most recent findings of science. The God of Scripture, of historic Judaism and Christianity, is essentially unknown to modern humankind. The images of an earlier generation have been largely distorted to portray God as an indulgent grandfather or an angry judge, and neither seems to have any relevance to a technological society. And science, on its part, purportedly has shown that we are alone in the unfeeling immensity of a universe to which we have come without plan or purpose, a mere accidental assemblage of molecules. But this is not what the current discoveries of science are telling us. The tight little mechanisms, the clockwork images, the strict following of cause by effect, the tangibility of matter, the gradual evolutionary climb, even our own objectivity, these and many more of the most familiar components of our credo are fading fast. Instead we find an exciting world in dynamic flux, an unexpected universe whose mechanisms are ever more baffling and staggering in their beauty and complexity, where predictability is uncertain instead of deterministic, where matter and energy are interchangeable, and where evolutionary change occurs by leaps and bounds that defy mechanistically simple explanation. And ourselves; what has become of us? The physicists tell us that we are peculiarly situated midway between the immense parameters of the cosmos and the infinitude of the smallest particles of matter and energy. Our arrival on this planet seems remarkable whether looked at in terms of the requirement for a special relationship among the forces controlling elementary particles, or in terms of the mechanisms of biological evolution. What is becoming increasingly obvious is that the evolutionary process that has resulted in humankind is a unique and unidirectional one. And the steps peculiar to Homo sapiens are remarkable in both their timing and their developmental aspects. We are a once-for-all happening, and, most wonderful of all, our journey has just begun.

THE THREE PHASES OF HUMAN DEVELOPMENT

One of the great benefits of examining the vast development of the cosmos is that by so doing we obtain a sufficiently broad perspective to begin to discern a purpose or plan—an ultimate meaning—in the evolutionary process. The alternative, by which science ordinarily functions, is to focus on limited components, detailing the processes and mechanisms involved. The risk of the latter is to see the process but miss the plan. It is for this reason that Sir John Eccles in his Gifford lectures of 1978 begins with the concept of the hierarchical structure of nature, in which higher levels are seen to emerge unpredictably from lower levels.[2] The example he uses is that of the emergence of life, which could not have been predicted even with complete knowledge of all the events of the prebiotic world. As we move on through hierarchies of increasing complexity, life gives rise to humankind, which itself then undergoes a leap to another hierarchy, consciousness. And conscious humankind next bounds to what we propose as an ultimate hierarchy: spiritual humankind. It is at this level that we see the greatest opportunity for humankind to develop those attributes that will allow the greatest harmony with each other and the greatest communion with the majestic and all-powerful Creator, into whose eternal purposes we fit. Perhaps our supernatural meaning will then be fully spelled out. We suspect that if and when that happens, we will have had the ultimate experience, the full vision of the awesome size of God. This book is, we hope, a beginning in that direction.

What we now know of the origins of humankind already hints at the awesome sweep of the Creator's hand. As Eiseley phrases it, this is "Nature's last great play—the play of man."[3] The role which the central character has assumed is a tremendously challenging one, for it embraces not only the ascent up the evolutionary ladder to a creature with unheard-of powers of mind and intellect, but also the advent of the uniquely human spiritual point of view.

PHYSICAL DEVELOPMENT

The physical phase of human evolution involves two great leaps upward, one at the point some two million years ago when our presumed ancestors—the Australopithecines—first walked erect, and the second at the advent of cultural humankind—Homo neandertals—with their greatly enlarged brain, perhaps 150,000 years ago. The period over which the brain increased threefold, from its one-pound weight in the hominid ancestor to three pounds in Homo sapiens, was amazingly brief, a time span totally unlike that in any other creature.

THE APPEARANCE OF INTELLECT

The large brain of Homo sapiens neandertal with its enlarged frontal lobes—in modern humans two times greater than in the chimpanzee—made possible an enormous capacity for cultural and intellectual development. Eccles points out that there were also accompanying qualitative changes in the so-called Broca and Wernicke speech centers of the brain that allowed for the development of language.[4] At this point the evolution of humankind turned a corner. No longer was physical size, even of the brain, a significant factor, as indicated by the fact that brain size has even decreased slightly from Homo sapiens neandertal to modern Homo sapiens. What happened instead was a vast and rapid change in cultural development. This was the phase of the intellect. Primitive humans began to plan their hunts, their defenses, their leadership. And these developments occurred just in the nick of time, for the open, grassy savannah was soon transformed into a sheet of ice as glaciers ground their way inexorably from the north. Toolmaking became sophisticated, symbols were developed for recordkeeping and for rituals associated with a developing social order, and people became artists. More than two hundred caves with exquisite drawings attest to the artistic sensitivity of prehistoric humankind.

What followed in civilized times was nothing short of miraculous. The rate of growth of our knowledge of our world was phenomenal. The pyramids of Egypt, the architecture of the Greek temples, the Roman aqueducts and roads, the world explorations by the Spanish and Portuguese, the great cathedrals of the Middle Ages: these were the products of human intellect. In our own century the acceleration of learning continues; indeed, more than half of the scientists who ever lived are alive today. More than half of the discoveries in the natural sciences have been made in this century. Half of the books ever written were written in this century. Intellect, like a grand invisible sphere surrounding our planet, has unleashed tremendous creative force in this last one-millionth of universal history.

THE SPIRITUALITY OF HUMANKIND

The most fascinating phase of the human journey is its spiritual development. There is strong evidence that early humans, Homo sapiens neandertals, protected the sick and crippled, buried their dead with reverence, and loved the animals whose pictures adorned their caves. This kinship of human and beast, this respect for both life and death went beyond mere concern for survival. It suggested that the daily tasks of hunting, caring for the young, preparing food and eating, could be interrupted for events of deeper meaning. But the crucial evidence regarding spirituality concerns the care of the dead, for in a number of instances it has been found that not only were the graves covered with flowers but there were tools and food and a ring of stones surrounding the dead, as though these would be needed in a future life. Thus even 100,000 years ago, humankind anticipated a hereafter!

Humanity's fascination with a spiritual dimension, a hidden sphere of power, an underlying ordering principle that lies unseen behind everyday events as well as gigantic happenings, has grown and taken on new importance in the ensuing centuries. Science has given us knowledge of the fundamental structure of matter in terms of a plethora of subatomic particles, and knowledge of processes of biology in terms of molecular mechanisms. But each new explanation seems to open up deeper questions, as though we still see only the outline of things and explain our observations by means of models that only approximate the truth. Indeed, many in science now see the limitations of scientific description and do not presume that scientific descriptions are ultimate truth. For some there is the added conviction that the Creator is revealing himself through science, so that the results of science serve as signs pointing to a larger Reality. But people cannot learn all about God by studying nature, because nature is only a contingent and partial manifestation of God. So we look to theology, particularly as it opens itself to the discoveries of science, to extend our knowledge of God. And so the sphere of the spirit will spread and energize new creative dimensions of understanding for future humankind.

THE CHANGING PATTERNS OF UNDERSTANDING OF THE CREATION

HUMANKIND'S AWE AND WONDER

Early humankind had a religious sense, an understanding that behind the awesome phenomena of nature—thunderstorms, floods, great animals, volcanic activity, whatever they saw—there were unseen forces at work. Their reaction has often been depicted as one of stark fear, but a little reflection will show that their experience was more a sense of awe and wonder. As the glacial ice receded under the summer sun, flowers bloomed and birds sang. There was a harmony in nature and now there was time and intelligence to reflect upon it, not unlike the way some American Indians relate to nature today.

POLYTHEISM AND GREEK PHILOSOPHY

Many of the awesome events observed by early humankind prompted their reverence, especially if the particular occurrence was beneficial for survival. Worship cults arose that centered on game animals and fertility deities. In a sense the worship of God became a pragmatic, materialistic phenomenon. By the time civilization reached the stage of the Egypt of the pyramids, polytheistic worship was the norm. It was so in southern Asia and in Greece and Rome as well. But the ancient Greeks gave us an additional dimension. They brought us not only the plethora of deities seen by St. Paul in ancient Athens, but also produced some of the most profound philosophical thinkers the world has ever known. The most influential from a scientific point of view was Aristotle, but unfortunately his philosophy and that of most of his fellows was dualistic, separating the human mind from the human body. The mind was seen as transcendent—almost Godlike—and was to be occupied with eternal ideas, such as truth, harmony, goodness, and beauty. The body, however, was of the earth and of less consequence. The tragic outcome of this dualism, in which things intelligible were considered of value but things of sense and feeling were viewed as meaningless, was the radical separation of theory from practice. It was this philosophical position that delayed empirical science until the incarnational thrust of Christianity affirmed the value of material things.

MONOTHEISM

Given the strength of polytheism, the monotheism of the Hebrews of the Old Testament is remarkable. Here arose, apparently from a Hebrew raised in the royal family and educational milieu of polytheistic Egypt, a powerful statement of the one God, maker of the heavens and Earth, at once Lord over all the forces of nature and the Creator of humankind. The power of that message swept the ancient world, and in the form of Christianity conquered pagan Rome and the rest of Europe. In the hands of the Muslim peoples, it swept across northern Africa and the Near East. In the Middle Ages it provided the foundation for some of the finest meditation and artistic expression our world has known. It also provided the foundation for empirical science.

MODERN SCIENCE

The Initial Openness to Theological Truth

There is strong support for the thesis that science arose as a consequence of a Judeo-Christian theology that viewed God as Creator and Supreme Ruler of nature, one who had not only brought the cosmos into being, but governed it by laws that reflected his faithfulness and consistency. The pioneers of science thus embarked on an unprecedented period of exploration with the attitude that God had given them a world to be understood and appreciated through science in much the way that theologians understood and appreciated God through the study of the Scriptures. This reverential attitude is seen in Francis Bacon, Isaac Newton, Clerk Maxwell, and the vast majority of their contemporaries. In this century it was profoundly the experience of Albert Einstein, of naturalist Louis Agassiz, and of physicist Werner Heisenberg. It is also the experience of neurophysiologist Sir John Eccles, and of astronomers Alan Sandage and Owen Gingerich.

The expectation of the early scientists that God would reveal himself in their endeavors was amply realized. With wonder they perceived intricate design and mathematical lawfulness everywhere they looked. And the result was a worship experience, a revelation of the profound nature of the vast universe, their own finitude, and the awesome size of God.

It is perhaps no better stated than in these words from Pascal's *Pensees,* written by the great scientist-theologian in 1657:

Let man then contemplate the whole of nature in her full and grand majesty, and turn his vision from the low objects which surround him. Let him gaze on that brilliant light, set like an eternal lamp to illumine the universe; let the earth appear to him a point in comparison with the vast circle described by the sun; and let him wonder at the fact that this vast circle is itself but a very fine point in comparison with that described by the stars in their revolution round the firmament. But if our view be arrested there, let our imagination pass beyond; it will sooner exhaust the power of conception than nature that of supplying material for conception. The whole visible world is only an imperceptible atom in the ample bosom of nature. No idea approaches it. We may enlarge our conceptions beyond all imaginable space; we only produce atoms in comparison with the reality of things. It is an infinite sphere, the centre of which is everywhere, the circumference nowhere. In short, it is the greatest sensible mark of the almighty power of God that imagination loses itself in that thought.

Returning to himself, let man consider what he is in comparison with all existence; let him regard himself as lost in this remote corner of nature; and from the little cell in which he finds himself lodged, I mean the universe, let him estimate at their true value the earth, kingdoms, cities, and himself. What is a man in the Infinite?

But to show him another prodigy equally astonishing, let him examine the most delicate things he knows. Let a mite be given him, with its minute body and parts incomparably more minute, limbs with their joints, veins in the limbs, blood in the veins, humours in the blood, drops in the humours, vapours in the drops. Dividing these last things again, let him exhaust his powers of conception, and let the last object at which he can arrive be now that of our discourse. Perhaps he will think that here is the smallest point of nature. I will let him see therein a new abyss. I will point for him not only the visible universe, but all that he can conceive of nature's immensity in the womb of this abridged atom. Let him see therein an infinity of universes, each of which has its firmament, its planets, its earth, in the same proportion as in the visible world; in each earth animals, and in the last mites, in which he will find again all that the first had, finding still in these others the same thing without end and without cessation. Let him lose himself in wonders as amazing in their littleness as the others in their vastness. For who will not be astounded at the fact that our body, which a little while ago was imperceptible in the universe, itself imperceptible in the bosom of the whole, is now a colossus, a world, or rather a whole, in respect of the nothingness which we cannot reach? He who regards himself in this light will be afraid of himself, and observing himself sustained in the body given him by nature between those two abysses of the Infinite and Nothing, will tremble at the sight of these marvels; and I think that, as his curiosity changes into admiration, he will be more disposed to contemplate them in silence than to examine them with presumption.[5]

Given this attitude among its practitioners, the first centuries of Western science were euphoric. People explored the creation with expectation and wonder, understanding that everything they observed was under the hand of Providence and thus contingent upon the divine will. And they were humbled before the size of God.

The Shift to a Conflict with Theology

Although the pioneers of science deemed nature an object worthy of study, there were others, in theology, who still remained influenced by the Greek dualistic ideas, which placed the Earth and things of sense and feeling below the considerations of mind and eternity. This worldview, which emphasized the perfection of God and heaven and Earth's baseness continued to be a source of friction between science and theology.

But this divisive force was joined in the seventeenth century by a second worldview, championed by two great scientists, Descartes and Newton, which emphasized God's immutability or unchanging faithfulness. Though both these great thinkers had no intention to undermine theology, the effect of their emphasis on God's timeless immutability was to separate his activity from his creation. For Descartes this meant that the ordinary interactions of created bodies that acted upon each other by the principle of inertia were independent of divine interventions. Thus all changes in natural processes since the initial creation were due to the interaction of finite things, not God. For Newton, God did continue to act in his creation, but through forces such as gravitation, which acted at a distance and were therefore not material. The consequence of the introduction of the principle of immutability was ironic, for neither Descartes nor Newton intended to emancipate the worldview of physics from the concept of God. But as the idea took hold that the universe operated like clockwork, by natural laws in which everything that occurred seemed resolvable into cause and effect, into action and reaction, the concept of God's activity became a problem, even an irritation. The result was an atheistic philosophical position called positivism, which viewed objective science as the successor to outmoded subjective metaphysical and religious philosophies.

The Modern Shift to Philosophical and Religious Openness

At the beginning of this century, the physicist Werner Heisenberg demonstrated a profound physical phenomenon: the uncertainty of the simultaneous knowledge of both position and momentum of elementary particles. The upshot of this was that events studied with individual subatomic particles seemed to have no bearing on the aggregate of particles in the macrocosm. The sum of the parts appeared to equal the whole, but without explanation. Then modern cosmology pointed to an enormous yet finite universe, which came to us by way of a "big bang," a singular event for which science had no explanation. Science was becoming much more open-ended.

On the biological side the study of the origin of life was growing increasingly confusing. What seemed abundantly obvious was that there is a delicate and intricate balance in the structure of the cosmos necessary for the emergence of life. The collection of constraints was so striking as to be given a name: the anthropic principle. If life came about by purely mechanistic means, then it was on the basis of a special sort of circumstance. As John Polkinghorne expresses it, "The closely knit character of a world containing life, which science begins to discern, suggests that it would not be as easy to tinker with things as we might have thought, assuming that some regularity and order are to underlie such a world."[6]

The scientific data base of this century also contains some remarkable findings on the human brain. The combination of all the neurons in a human brain and the multitude of connections between neurons makes for a level of complexity that rivals the number of stars in the universe. In effect, there is a universe of complexity in each of our heads! Such complexity appears to be arising everywhere.

The critical breakthrough in the movement back to theological openness came with the publication of Michael Polanyi's philosophical treatise entitled *Personal Knowledge.* [7] What Polanyi suggests is that even scientists bring to their theorizing a commitment to truth or at least potential truth. And it is his powerful conclusion that even in science there is no such thing as abstract knowledge. It is always knowledge held by someone as a commitment. It involves the whole person and that person's passionate contribution to the personal act of knowing. The idea of strict objectivity in science is thus open to serious question. Of course as data gatherers, scientists should be careful to be as objective as possible. But any idea that the end result of their theorizing is pure, objective truth is simply mistaken.

The modern shift in science is to theological openness. There are pockets of resistance here and there; the molecular geneticists are still largely clinging to determinism because of the enormous explanatory power of the DNA revolution. But cracks are beginning to show even in this part of the once-splendid edifice of objectivity. For example, the aforementioned study of the origin of life reveals ever-larger problems to surmount. As pointed out recently by biochemist Robert Shapiro, it is beginning to look very open-ended in all of science.[8] Physicist Paul Davies says, "Science offers a surer path to God than religion."[9]

MODERN THEOLOGICAL CONSERVATISM AND THE BEGINNINGS OF OPENNESS

The irony of present events is that although many scientists are moving toward a position of openness to philosophical and religious questions, the theological establishment is largely still entrenched in a conservative posture like that of their counterparts of past centuries. Few seminaries or university theology departments seem interested in genuine dialogue with the scientific community. But several centers have begun to develop outside the usual academic structures both in the United States and in Britain. The Center for Theological Inquiry at Princeton, headed by former Princeton Theological Seminary President James McCord, and The Center for Theology and the Natural Sciences in Berkeley, California, headed by Robert Russell, are developing good programs. The Ian Ramsey Center at Oxford University in England, headed by Arthur Peacocke, of St. Cross College, is also drawing scholars together from theology and the sciences. Other organizations that are promoting the interaction of science and theology are the American Scientific Affiliation in Ipswich, Massachusetts, the Institute for Theological Encounter with Science and Technology in St. Louis, the Science and Religion Forum at Derby, England, and Christians in Science of Leicester, England. Several outstanding conservative theologians have been involved with the Princeton Center, including Seton Hall Jesuit theologian-scientist Stanley Jaki and University of Edinburgh Emeritus Professor of Theology Thomas Torrance. Both are prolific writers and both have been recipients of the Templeton Prize for Progress in Religion. But what of the future? Ralph Wendell Burhoe, founding editor of *Zygon: Journal of Religion and Science* (and another Templeton Prize winner), prophesies that the impact of a growing group of scientific seers will be to significantly confirm and extend religious faith, thereby gaining the confidence of theologians, and leading to an enlarged vision and purpose for human beings. The overall picture is one of fascinating opportunity for theological progress, as the sphere of the spirit extends to new horizons. But Rustum Roy of Pennsylvania State University sees the issue differently. As he states in his book *Experimenting with Truth,* [10] we must begin to see God in closer association with the material world of science and technology. But God is not to be confused with the world, as in some pantheist construction; Roy proposes instead the *panentheistic* approach. God is the essence that we approach from reality, his manifold material expressions, through understanding. The thrust of this kind of construction is that we once more begin to intimately identify the awesome universe in its every shape and manifestation with the God who is its essence. And we begin to experience the size of God.

RECENT SCIENTIFIC DEVELOPMENTS AND THE REVELATION OF GOD

Our thesis is that God is revealing himself in all his immensity at an ever-accelerating pace through rapid developments in the sciences. The sphere of the spirit is expanding exponentially all across the scientific landscape. Among the most prominent features are the fields of cosmogony—the study of the origin of the universe—and of molecular biology. In between these two extremes of the galactic and the molecular stand two other prominent areas of rapid development: the studies of universal order and of human evolution.

In the rapidly proliferating research areas of cosmogony new theories are under construction about pulsars and black holes, about other possible universes and about the origin of this one. In molecular biology the geneticists are busily reconfiguring the genome of simple organisms to account for phenomena such as transposons and mutator genes, and researchers in the study of life's origin are struggling over the source of the code upon which present-known life depends. In the study of universal order, it is observed, quite unexpectedly, that there are deep and powerful ordering forces in the universe. This is especially observed in recent developments in the study of what are called far-from-equilibrium processes, in which it is seen that there are spontaneous transitions within apparently random processes to higher levels of order. One might presume to say that there is a wholeness to the universe that cannot be broken! And finally, when we come to the most recent data for human evolution, we are surprised by the high intelligence of our ancestors of 200,000 years, and the rapidity with which this sphere of intelligence expanded with remarkable innovation and discovery, artistic expression and technology. It was as though some unseen force was unleashed with the advent of the human—the toolmaker, the burier of the dead. No creature like this had ever crawled on this Earth, much less strode across it on two legs!

The aggregate of these momentous developments in science, which we will deal with in detail, and a plethora of findings in numerous other areas of science, some of which will be sketched out in the final chapter, serve to signal that a new order—the sphere of the spirit—is coming. In this new order further exploration will open ever more strange and wonderful visions of what we, and our universe, are, and what we may become.

THE JOURNEY OF FAITH AND THE MAGNITUDE OF GOD

It is our conviction that the exploration of God's universe that is just beginning will become a new journey of faith, a voyage into the sphere of the spirit. As we see it, our journey began billions of years ago in the aftermath of that blinding detonation when the universe began. It has since followed the twists and turns of an amazing evolutionary process involving such diverse phenomena as supernovae and biogenesis, stromatolites and animal extinctions, cave drawings and pyramids. Then, after the remarkable advent of monotheism, God revealed himself in a Person, Jesus Christ, in what Christianity calls the Incarnation.

Here was God's great expression of love and interest in his creatures, and for fifteen centuries it remained the preoccupation of, and fulfillment for, the faithful. Granted, for some the Incarnation meant that God had come into his world to give new meaning to matter and humankind. The mundane things of time and sense were important. The world, though fallen, was still good. But for the vast majority of believers in medieval times, the material world had lost its significance; it served only as a stage prop for the drama of salvation.

The tragedy of our times is that the faithful are still preoccupied with the immediate significance of the Incarnation in terms of personal salvation, crucial though that is, but understand nothing of its theological significance in terms of the vast design of God in Creation. Yet the incarnate Christ is put before us in Scripture as the Creator and Sustainer of the universe.[11] His coming to Earth affirms that he is continuing to reveal to the hearts and minds of humankind the true meaning of the Creation He has made. Could not the Incarnation have been also a picture of what God was doing in Creation, linking the spiritual and material in the long and tortuous path of evolution from stardust to praying humanity? Did Earth's spiritual history consummate in the Incarnation, or was it also the beginning of a new era, in which the fallen Adam of Genesis 3[12] could become once again the Viceroys of God, the steward over the Creation!?

We considered earlier how the pioneers of science began to emulate this character as they approached the "book of God's works" on their knees, prostrate at the wonders of God's Creation. Then for a long time, science made itself an object of worship, and God was forgotten. But now in our time, people are again beginning to find fresh spiritual food in their study of the awesome cosmos. And they are finding God to be the Great Revealer, the God Who Would Be Known! Consider the opportunities that lie before us to see the great unfolding of the cosmos as a vast tapestry, woven through with the message of the awesome Creator, the Author and Finisher of our faith. The universe does indeed have meaning and purpose, and we can *read the message.* The implications for our science of this attitude of faith are staggering. For example, consider what we may learn of the power of love examined not in Freudian unbelief, but with openness to the spiritual message that "God is love."[13] Again, think of hope. Is it really just a psychological projection of unmet need, or could it be a God-given resource for the mobilization of inner strength? Then consider inner peace. The Scripture again gives us a valuable spiritual lesson that science should explore at great depth. In Luke 8 Jesus was asleep below while the disciples' fishing boat was tossed by an angry storm. In fear of their lives they awakened him with the words, "Master, Master, we are perishing." Jesus' response was to "rebuke the wind and the raging waters," and then we are told "the storm subsided and all was calm."[14] What was the difference? Clearly Jesus' power and deity were manifest, but there is another powerful lesson here. The disciples had seen the turmoil around them and were paralyzed with fear. The turmoil outside became turmoil inside. Jesus, by contrast, drew from the peace within himself and brought peace to the turmoil without.

Are there physiological and psychosomatic correlates to these desirable attributes? Can our science help to make them more intelligible or attainable? Can we begin to think more holistically? Is our science powerful enough to begin to piece together the complexity of the human dimensions of physical, intellectual, and spiritual life? We think so. We think that the science of the future will be filled with possibilities to enrich our spiritual understanding. The primary prerequisite is an openness to seeing beyond our instruments and theorems, our personal successes and aspirations, to the glorious plan and the enormity of the Planner. The hymn writer Arthur Campbell Ainger says it well:

> God is working his purpose out
> As year succeeds to year
> God is working his purpose out
> And the time is drawing near;
> Nearer and nearer draws the time,
> the time that shall surely be,
> When the earth shall be filled with
> the glory of God
> As the waters cover the sea.[15]

NOTES

1. Acts 17:22–25. Holy Bible, New International Version.
2. Sir John C. Eccles, *The Human Mystery* (London: Routledge and Kegan Paul, 1984), 9–10.

3. Loren Eiseley, *The Invisible Pyramid* (New York: Charles Scribner & Sons, 1970), 18.
4. Eccles, *The Human Mystery,* 90.
5. Blaise Pascal, *Pensees Great Books of the Western World* Vol. 33. Ecyclopedia Brittanica (Chicago, 1952), 181.
6. John Polkinghorne, *The Way the World Is* (Grand Rapids: Eerdmans, 1986), 13.
7. Michael Polanyi, *Personal Knowledge* (New York: Harper Torchbooks, Harper & Row, 1966).
8. Robert Shapiro, *Origins: A Skeptic's Guide to the Creation of Life on Earth* (New York: Summit Books, 1986).
9. Paul Davies, *God and the New Physics* (New York: Simon & Schuster, 1983), ix.
10. Rustum Roy, *Experimenting with Truth* (Oxford: Pergamon Press, 1981).
11. Heb. 1:3, NIV.
12. Gen. 3:1–19, NIV.
13. 1 John 4:8, NIV.
14. Luke 8:22–25, RSV.
15. Arthur Campbell Ainger, "The Church's Mission," *The Hymnal 1982* (New York: The Church Hymnal Corp., 1982).

2. Science Expands Our Understanding of Nature and Reality

A SUCCESSION OF WORLDVIEWS

James Houston, writing in *I Believe in the Creator,* points out that in the history of Western civilization, two worldviews have profoundly influenced both our thought and our theology. The first was the Ptolemaic worldview, a synthesis of Platonic dualism and Christian faith, which "deepened the split in human culture between the celestial and the terrestrial, the ideal and the sensible, the supernatural and the natural, the spiritual and the material." The second worldview, the Newtonian, was ushered in by early scientists in the seventeenth century, devout people of God such as Copernicus, Kepler, Galileo, and Newton.[1] Unintentionally, they provided philosophers and theologians with a universe as mechanical as a clock, apparently closed to the concerns of its Creator, operating autonomously and mechanically.

The effect that these two worldviews have had upon human culture is great. Philip Yancey, writing in *Christianity Today,* says that even in our day, "Christian writers express their theological concepts without emotion, drama, or tension," because of a low view of God's Creation. He says,

G. K. Chesterton proposed a theory to explain the Dark Ages, that wasteland of painting, music, writing, and the other arts. Could they, he asked, be a necessary interlude after the Roman and Greek defilement and before the discovery of the true Romance? Nature had, in fact, been spoiled. "It was no good telling such people to have a natural religion full of stars and flowers. There was not even a flower or a star that had not been stained.

They had to go into the desert, the monasteries, where they could find no flowers or even into the cavern where they could see no stars . . . Pan was nothing but panic. Venus was nothing but venereal vice."

Gradually against this gray background beauty began to appear, something fresh and delicate. In Saint Francis of Assisi, the flowers and stars recovered their first innocence, fire and water were deemed worthy to be the brother and sister of a saint. The purge of paganism was complete at last, and Christians began to rediscover nature with a rush. The greatest blossoming of art in all of history, the Renaissance, immediately followed.

Several centuries later, however, the scientific revolution sent new shock waves through the church, from which we have not yet recovered. Nature and supernature split apart. The church abandoned nature to the physicists, and geologists, and biologists, retreating to the more limited purlieu of theological speculation. The scientists, in turn, abandoned the supernatural to the church and the paranormalists.

Too often today Christian writers tiptoe around God's creation; it is simply "matter," unworthy of the attention granted supernatural issue. (Similarly, says Jacques Ellul, science avoids questions of supernature to such an extent that it puts on blinders and severely restricts intellectual thought.) It is time for Christian writers to rediscover our natural environment and the characteristics of true humanity. By avoiding nature we divorce ourselves from the greatest images and carriers of supernature, and our writing loses its chief advantage, the ability to mimic creation. When Tolstoy describes spring, the wonder of tiny flowers poking up through the thawing tundra, he invests in it the same exuberance and significance that he gives to a description of Christian conversion. It too is an expression of God's world.[2]

But something has been happening in the past few decades of this century. Science appears to be leading us back to a profound respect and an expansive attitude toward nature. God's activity has been seen to be far more open-ended and immediate than the clockwork image would allow. The realization has been expressed by scientists of widely differing theological persuasions using a variety of thought models.

MODELS OF NATURE AND REALITY

In recent years theologians and scientists have provided us with a rich variety of ways in which the relationship between Nature and its Creator and Sustainer may be better depicted. Arthur Peacocke has reviewed some of the theological models in *Cosmology, History and Theology:*

A number of complementary and reinforcing models have been necessary to avoid the extreme of a completely transcendent God (merging into deism) and of a completely immanent God (merging into pantheism). In deism God has no effective interaction with the world; and in pantheism God tends to be identified with the world—and the Christian idea of creation repudiates both extremes. The models which have been used in the past range from those stressing transcendence and the distance between Creator and creation (such as God as Maker, closely related to God as King and Sovereign) to those stressing the close and intimate relation between Creation and Creator (e.g., the relation of breath to a body, or parts of a living organism to the whole). Some modern authors have furthermore seen relevant analogies in the relation of an artist to his work and the process-theologians have espoused the term "panentheism" to denote a doctrine which attempts to combine transcendence and immanence by asserting that the world is "in" God, but that his being is not exhausted by the world. Biblical images have included the thought of creation as like a garment worn by God; as like the work of a potter; as a kind of emanation of God's life-giving energy, or spirit; as the manifestation of God's Wisdom (Sophia) or Word (Logos), which are hypostatized so that they represent the outgoing being and action of God in creation from within his own inner and ineffable nature.[3]

GOD, THE COSMIC ARTIST

Donald MacKay, British biophysicist and world authority on brain physiology, presents one of the theological models that emphasizes immanence in his *Science and Christian Faith Today:*

The Bible as a whole represents God in far too intimate and active a relationship to daily events to be represented in . . . mechanical terms. He does not come in only at the beginning of time to "wind up the works";

he continually "upholds all things by the word of His power" (Hebrews 1.3). "In Him" (i.e. Christ) "all things hold together" (Colossians 1.17). Here is an idea radically different from that of tending or interfering with a machine. It is not only the physically inexplicable happenings (if any), but the whole going concern, that the Bible associates with the constant activity of God. . . . The whole multi-patterned drama of our universe is declared to be continually "held in being" and governed by Him.[4]

MacKay goes on to suggest the activity of God to be more like that of an artist than a machine: tender. He says,

An imaginative artist brings into being a world of his own invention. He does it normally by laying down patches of paint on canvas, in a certain spatial order (or disorder!). The order which he gives the paint determines the form of the world he invents. Imagine now an artist able to bring his world into being, not by laying down paint on canvas, but by producing an extremely rapid succession of sparks of light on the screen of a television tube. (This is in fact the way in which a normal television picture is held in being.) The world he invents is now not static but dynamic, able to change and evolve at his will. Both its form and its laws of change (if any) depend on the way in which he orders the sparks of light in space and time. With one sequence he produces a calm landscape with quietly rolling clouds; with another, we are looking at a vigorous cricket match on a village green. The scene is steady and unchanging just for as long as he wills it so; but if he were to cease his activity, his invented world would not become chaotic; it would simply cease to be.

The God in whom the Bible invites belief is no "Cosmic Mechanic." Rather is He the Cosmic Artist, the creative Upholder, without whose continual activity there would be not even chaos, but just nothing. What we call physical laws are expressions of the regularity that we find in the pattern of created events that we study as the physical world. Physically, they express the nature of the entities "held in being" in the pattern. Theologically, they express the stability of the great Artist's creative will. Explanations in terms of scientific laws and in terms of divine activity are thus not rival answers to the same question; yet they are not talking about different things. They are (or at any rate purport to be) complementary accounts of different aspects of the same happening, which in its full nature cannot be adequately described by either alone.[5]

THE COSMIC RELIGIOUS FEELING: UNITY AND ORDER

Beyond the strictly biblical viewpoint lies a whole range of thought models that also seek to define Nature and Reality. Most of them challenge our limited appreciation for the awesome intricacy and multidimensionality of the force behind the universe.

Almost without peer in the scientific world, Albert Einstein brought about a revolution in physics in this century. In the theory of special relativity, he showed the equivalence of mass and energy, and in general relativity he showed the indivisibility of the space-time continuum. He attributed much of his success and motivation to a fervent belief in the ultimate unity and order of the universe. The goal of his later years was the production of a unified field theory, in which all the forces of the universe would be interrelated. As Lincoln Barnett describes it,

His Unified Field Theory sought to culminate and climax this coalescing process. For from its august perspective the entire universe appears as one elemental field in which each star, each atom, each wandering comet and slow-wheeling galaxy and flying electron is seen to be but a ripple or tumescence in the underlying space-time unity. And so a profound simplicity would supplant the surface complexity of nature. The distinctions between gravitational force and electromagnetic force, matter and energy, electric charge and field, space and time, all fade in the light of their revealed relationships and resolve into configurations of the four-dimensional continuum which Einstein revealed the universe to be. Thus all man's perceptions of the world and all his abstract intuitions of reality would merge finally into one, and the deep underlying unity of the universe would be laid bare.[6]

The religious sense of this revelation is emphasized by the fact that there was not in this quest for unity and simplicity any hint of arrogance or superiority in Einstein. He was, as he said on many occasions, awed by the infinite intelligence, by a deep sense of its mysteriousness, and by the staggering fact of the comprehensibility of the universe. Stanley Jaki, in his *Road of Science and the Ways to God,* quotes a letter from Einstein to his friend Maurice Solovine:

"You find it surprising," he wrote to Solovine on March 30, 1952, "that I think of the comprehensibility of the world (insofar as we are entitled to speak of such world) as a miracle or an eternal mystery. But surely, a priori, one should expect the world to be chaotic, not to be grasped by thought in any way. One might (indeed one *should*) expect that the world evidenced itself as lawful only so far as we grasp it in an orderly fashion. This would be a sort of order like the alphabetical order of words. On the other hand, the kind of order created, for example, by Newton's gravitational theory is of a very different character. Even if the axioms of the theory are posited by man, the success of such a procedure supposed in the objective world a high degree of order, which we are in no way entitled to expect a priori. Therein lies the 'miracle' which becomes more and more evident as our knowledge develops." To this Einstein added the even more revealing remark: "And here is the weak point of positivists and of professional atheists, who feel happy because they think that they have preempted not only the world of the divine but also of the miraculous. Curiously, we have to be resigned to recognizing the 'miracle' without having any legitimate way of getting any further. I have to add the last point explicitly, lest you think that weakened by age I have fallen into the hands of priests."[7]

Einstein failed in his ultimate scientific aim, which was to produce a unified field theory. But, as Jaki goes on to say,

He failed, but there was an Einsteinian greatness in his failure. It was not unclear to him that success demanded more than simplicity of equations. He tried many of them, often making the comment that they were so beautifully simple that God himself would not have passed them over. But he also knew that beyond simplicity of forms there was need for a simplicity of principles, like the ones that guided him in connection with special and general relativity. Far more important, he knew in the measure in which the true physiognomy of his creative science had become clear to him that those principles had to relate to an objectively existing totality of things, or the universe. Such a universe was not the creation of the mind, nor could its high degree of order be expected a priori. The orderly world was something given.[8]

Furthermore, Einstein seems to have attributed much of his scientific success to the interaction of experimental data and creative imagination, with the latter component recognized again as something given. This aspect is touched on by Iain Paul in *Science, Theology and Einstein:*

Einstein was far too good a scientist, too profound a thinker, to forget for one moment the mystery of the inseparability of the empirical and theoretical components of knowledge. This mystery, for example, lies at the heart of the general theory of relativity and at the core of determinate nature. That is why Einstein prefaced the above advice with the following statement. "To him who is a discoverer in this field [theoretical physics], the products of his imagination appear as so necessary and natural that he regards them, and would like to have them regarded by others, not as creations of thought but as given realities."[9]

It would seem that Einstein's God takes on some of the biblical character of the Giver of Light, the Great Revealer, who rejoices when any of the vast truth of the creation is brought to light and obeyed in humility.

NATURAL LAW AS VANISHING LINES INTO THE ETERNAL ORDER

God is the great Revealer, and it would seem that the natural world is so constituted that its laws point not only to an orderly universe but also beyond, to an unseen eternal order. So wrote Henry Drummond a century ago in his book *Natural Law in the Spiritual World:*

The natural Laws then are great lines running not only through the world, but, as we now know, through the universe, reducing it like parallels of latitude to intelligent order. In themselves, be it once more repeated, they may have no more absolute existence than parallels of latitude. But they exist for us. They are drawn for us to understand the part by some Hand that drew the whole; so drawn, perhaps, that understanding the part, we too in time may learn to understand the whole. Now the inquiry we propose to ourselves resolves itself into the simple question, Do these lines stop with what we call the natural sphere? Is it not possible that they may lead further? Is it probable that the Hand which ruled them gave up the work where most of all they were required? Did that Hand divide the world into two, a cosmos, and a chaos, the higher being the chaos? With Nature being the symbol of all of harmony and beauty that is known to man, must we still talk of the super-natural, not as a convenient word, but as a different order of world, an unintelligible world, where the Reign of Mystery supersedes the Reign of Law? In discussing the relations of the Natural and Spiritual kingdom, it has been all but implied hitherto that the Spiritual laws were framed originally on the plan of the Natural; and the impression one might receive in studying the two worlds for the first time from the side of analogy would naturally be that the lower world was formed first, as a kind of scaffolding on which the higher and spiritual should be afterwards raised. Now the exact opposite has been the case. The first in the field was the Spiritual world. The physical properties of matter form the alphabet which is put into our hands by God, the study of which, if properly conducted, will enable us more perfectly to read that great book which we call the Universe. But, over and above this, the Natural Laws will enable us to read that great duplicate which we call the "Unseen Universe," and to think and live in fuller harmony with it. After all, the true greatness of Law lies in its vision of the Unseen. Law in the visible is the Invisible in the visible. And to speak of Laws as Natural is to define them in their application to a part of the universe, the sense-part, whereas a wider survey could lead us to regard all Law as essentially Spiritual. To magnify the Laws of Nature, as Laws of this small world of ours, is to take a provincial view of the universe. Law is great not because the phenomenal world is great, but because these vanishing lines are the avenues into the eternal order.[10]

Nature, then, is seen as a continuum, beginning in the spiritual realm and proceeding in the form of what we call natural law into the visible. From the natural side our powers of comprehension are limited, because nature is only a contingent and partial manifestation of God. But as science yields more and more data about the universe, we see that in fact God is revealing himself more and more to human inquiry.

PANENTHEISM

More recent views of nature stress an even more direct or intimate association between the natural and the spiritual. Rustum Roy, Pennsylvania State University geochemist, in his book *Experimenting with Truth,* asserts that "no significant advance in theology will ever be made again by any religious Tradition in any part of the world unless the basic insights of science and technology are

fully integrated into it." For this full integration Roy proposes that
we start by eliminating the word *God*, which is so encumbered
with the negative feelings of the secular community, and sub-
stituting in our writing a collection of tiny printed dots, which
would mean "cloud of essence." (Wil Lepkowski, whose review of
Roy's book is published in *Chemical and Engineering News*, suggests
the symbol ***.)[11] For his theology Roy proposes a "scientifically
elaborated panentheism," which he describes as "the view that
'***' is known or expressed *through* all Reality . . . the enthusiastic
affirmation of '***,' present and manifest to us *through everything*";
and that there is no way to " '***' except *through*—through the
world, nature, spring flowers, fall leaves, friends, mother, prayer,
Jesus, pi-mesons, cups of cold water, and nuclear fireballs. Pantheism is a very different matter. Pantheism *equates* everything with
'***.' "

To illustrate the difference between panentheism and pantheism, Roy presents a parable about sweetness. The story is one of
anthropologists observing that different tribes in various parts of
the world discovered that different plants exhibited the taste sensation of sweetness. Each tribe found sweetness in a different
thing: one tribe found it in strawberries, another in raspberries, a
third in sugar cane, a fourth in honey. Each assumed its source was
the valid one, and other sources were to be rejected. Ages passed
and the list of "local vehicles" for sweetness grew. Then a new
report came that a Semitic sect in the eastern Mediterranean had
found the "common denominator of all these forms." It had succeeded in crystallizing out a single substance, sugar, which could
sweeten any food. But, Roy explains,

The man who had crystallized out the sugar insisted that sugar was still
only an "incarnation," that sweetness was the only reality. Sweetness was
infinitely more satisfying than sugar or any of the local berries or canes.
He and his disciples preached that what was important was to search for
the essence of "sweetness" in all foods, in all cultures and circumstances.
They urged all to pursue the essence and the idea, and not a particular
form, not even sugar "itself."

The remainder of the parable is a tale of declension and eventual recovery. The distinctions between sweet foods, sugar, and sweetness began to be blurred. Then suddenly the secret of making sugar was lost, and the tribe that had discovered it, though struggling valiantly to keep the memory of this purest form of sweetness alive, gradually turned to the worship of one of the other sources of sweetness, beet roots.

In the end, after bouts with mind control and artificial sweeteners—saccharines and cyclamates—the various tribes came together and agreed that

it was really the experience, the sensation of Sweetness (also called God) which was the highest goal. All agreed that sweetness can be experienced only by consuming some real substance; and that many such substances exist, each called a religion, each adapted more or less to its environment. Most agreed that even artificial sweeteners contribute to our experience of sweetness, though there is for the human (= natural) condition a rather pure form of realized sweetness: sugar. Sugar was seen as the molecular embodiment (incarnation?) of sweetness, and the agent of sweetness camouflaged in the entire range of berries, roots and canes.

In applying the parable to the comparison of panentheism and pantheism, Roy explains that

to a pantheist strawberries, sugarcane, beets and sugar are all "theos." To a pan-en-theist the theos is sweetness which may be experienced through strawberries, sugarcane, beets or sugar. . . . The relation of the sensation of sweetness to sugar and, thence, to a variety of fruits is an introduction to the topic of embodiment or incarnation of "ideas," or principles of any abstract concept. The connection between "***" and reality is mirrored in the relationship of sweetness to sugarcane. To get to "***" one must *go through reality.* [12]

Scientific panentheism was pioneered as a concept by Pierre Teilhard de Chardin. What he emphasizes is that God may be found through all of the real world of things, experiences, and ideas; that God is the essence of all reality. What is needed, Roy contends, is a deeper understanding of the relationship between reality and God. Meaning is required to connect the two, so that the path of understanding is "Reality—meaning—essence." Artists have helped us with this understanding. The American artist Ben Shahn has written about these ideas in his book *The Shape of Content.* Based upon Shahn's artistic perspective, Roy writes,

Reality is reification—the turning of God into a material entity, rendering God accessible to others, giving it permanence, willing it to the race. The reality is as varied as are the accidental meetings of nature. Reality in religion is as varied as idea itself.

It is the visible shape of all man's growth; it is the living picture of his tribe at its most primitive, and of his civilization at its most sophisticated state. Religious reality is the many faces of the legend; it includes the infinite images of art; it is the expression and remnant of self. Reality is the very shape of God.

But because reality is the expression of God in material form, it is necessarily, even in its most awesome form, only a partial view of what God is. Roy goes on:

For Reality is not just the intentions of God, it is the embodiment of God. All reality is based first on some aspect, some theme of God. Reality is, second, a marshalling of materials, the inert matter in which the theme is to be cast. Reality is, third, a setting of boundaries or limits, the whole extent or a part of God but no more, the outer shape of God. All reality is thus disciplining, a limitation, an ordering of God to be manifest in one place at one time to a particular person. It can be said with certainty that any reality that emerges cannot be greater than the God which "went into it." For reality is only the manifestation, the shape of God.

Roy's conclusion:

"***" is that which Reality betrays but does not parade.[13]

The result of this understanding and its development in the life of Teilhard is notable. His brief testimony, from *An Album,* reads

Throughout my life, by means of my life, the world has little by little caught fire in my sight until, aflame all around me, it has become almost completely luminous from within. . . . Such has been my experience in contact with the earth—the diaphaneity of the Divine at the heart of the universe on fire . . . Christ; his heart; a fire; capable of penetrating every-where and, gradually, spreading everywhere.[14]

Finally, Roy chides many in the scientific community for ignoring this intimate experience of the transcendent God that is possible when we study the material world. He says,

While scientists all over the world prattle somewhat naively about beauty in science, hinting in a vague way that the true and the beautiful must be consistent, most have not spent a tenth as much intellectual energy on what is surely at least an equally important premise and vastly more significant to the human condition, namely, that the true and the good must be closely interwoven.[15]

THE THOUGHT MODEL

A wonderful statement about God is given in the first chapter of John. In the majestic language of the King James version it reads, "In the beginning was the Word and the Word was with God and the Word was God. All things were made through him, and without Him was not anything made that was made. In him was life, and the life was the light of men."[16] This might be paraphrased in the language of modern science as, "God is Creator of the universe of time and of humankind. Creation proceeds from idea to word to sense data. The Creator is not completely visible but is the Universal Spirit, the causative Idea which sustains and dwells in all He created and is creating. The orderliness and lawfulness of nature and of spirit exhibit God to humankind."

Biblical commentators have pondered the meaning of *Word*. In the Greek the term means "a thought" or "a concept" or "the expression or utterance of a thought." Others have suggested that *Word* is "the all-pervading concept."

Nineteenth-century writers captured this same idea. Vissarion Belinski writes, "God's whole boundless and beautiful world is the breath of one eternal idea, the thought of one eternal God."[17]

And the poet John Stuart Blackie says,

> Of sphere harmonious linked to sphere,
> In endless bright array.

> All that far-reaching Science there
> Can measure with her rod,
> All powers, all laws, are but the fair
> Embodied thoughts of God.[18]

The proposal that the Creator is expressed as thought or concept is especially fascinating in the light of ideas on the nature of matter and energy in the post-Einsteinian world. The British physicist James Jeans writes,

Today there is a wide measure of agreement, which on the physical side of science approaches almost to unanimity, that the stream of knowledge is heading towards a non-mechanical reality. The universe begins to look more like a great thought than like a great machine. Mind no longer appears as an accidental intruder into the realm of matter. We ought rather to hail it as the creator and governor of the realm of matter.[19]

The ideas of the universe as a great thought and of mind as Creator provide an interesting correlation to those astounding observations of the physicists concerning the delicate balancing of the cosmological parameters to allow for the evolution of intelligent life. Recalling Henry Simmons's words:

The value of the gravitational coupling seems precisely poised to permit the evolution of a particular universe. This universe must contain short-lived, metal-scattering, blue-giant stars; long-lived, evenly burning, slowly turning stars such as the sun; and observers.[20]

Observers, human observers, intelligence destined by some grand design to be here, on this tiny planet in one of a myriad of galaxies. Creator, as mind, creating mind! The alternative, a mindless universe, seems absurd.

Joseph Wood Krutch, in his *The Great Chain of Life,* writes of the staggering supposition "that human consciousness could have arisen from the 'merely material.'"

To say "I am a materialist" is meaningful only if the term "matter" can be defined in such a way as to distinguish it from something else. Until a few years ago such a definition seemed easy. "Matter is that which occupies space and has weight." This definition distinguished it as clearly from "energy," which occupies no space, as it does from such vaguer terms as "life" or "spirit" or "idea," which, having neither the characteristics of matter nor, demonstrably, the characteristics of energy, were sometimes assumed either to be an obscure form of energy or not to exist at all. To say "I am a materialist" meant, "I believe that the only fundamental reality is that which occupies space and which has weight."

But the matter that disintegrated privately over the American desert and then publicly over Japan ceased in those instants to occupy space. At those instants, therefore, the meaning of the term "materialist" disappeared as completely as the disintegrated atoms themselves. Between the man who says "I am a materialist because everything is ultimately material" and the man who says "I am not a materialist because nothing is ultimately material" no definable difference any longer exists.

On the basis of this seemingly demonstrated fact, many a scientific treatise will have to be revised if the now meaningless statements are to be removed from them. Almost at random I open a recent book on one of the biological sciences. The authority of a distinguished scientist is quoted to support the contention that the first appearance of life on earth may be accounted for "without the intervention of the non-material." In the light of the most recent knowledge does this statement mean anything at all?

Such speculations as these at least remind us of the astonishing fact that after this earth had existed for billions of years there finally appeared upon it a creature capable of abstract thought, interested in such philosophical questions as science raises, and bold enough to be able, or at least fancy that he is able, to reach back through billions of years to form what he believes to be more or less correct opinions concerning what happened so long ago.

If it really is true that he is merely the inevitable culmination of an improbable chemical reaction which happened to take place once and once only and involved "merely material" atoms, then the fact that he has been able to formulate the idea of "an improbable chemical reaction" and to trace himself back to it is remarkable indeed. That chemicals which are "merely material" should come to understand their own nature is a staggering supposition. Is it also a preposterous one?

Without attempting to answer that last question one thing more may be said. If it should turn out that man has not understood but misunderstood his own evolution then that is still a fact almost as staggering as understanding it would be. But it is also a staggering irony.

If, to go one step farther, the misunderstanding should lead him to deny, disregard, and allow to atrophy through disuse the very characteristics and powers which most distinguish him—if, in a word, he should thus help himself back down the road he once came up—that would be more than a staggering fact and more than a staggering irony. It would be of all calamities one of the greatest that could befall him—greater perhaps than any except that possibility of falling into the hands of an angry god he once so much feared.[21]

FROM SCIENCE TO SPIRIT

Much evidence indicates that we are now entering the sphere of the spirit. Great minds are beginning to see the reality that lies behind fleeting appearances. Most scientists say the universe started roughly eighteen billion years ago with a big bang. Then for about 80 percent of the history of the universe nothing existed but minerals. Then in the latest one-fifth of history, the sphere of life began.

On a little planet called Earth, a thin sphere of life began. To anyone trying to observe this life from another star or another galaxy it would be invisible, and such an observer might say it did not exist. But we who are part of this life sphere can see that for a billion years, tens of thousands of plants and insects and animals have developed in miraculous ways.

Now, in the latest one-millionth of universal history, the sphere of life has become enveloped by the sphere of intellect. Intellect, too, is invisible. You might have a hard time explaining to someone in another solar system what intellect is. You cannot see it in a telescope, you cannot weigh it, and nobody really knows what it is, even here. Since humans learned to read and write about ten thousand years ago, the sphere of the intellect has spread all over the world and become a tremendous creative force. Without this sphere of intellect we would not be able to have one hundred times as much energy working for us as our ancestors did two centuries ago. Without this sphere of intellect we would not have books or science or the richness of life. This sphere of the intellect is an invisible envelope that has recently surrounded our planet.

We are beginning to see evidence of a new sphere outside the sphere of intellect, which may be called the sphere of the spirit. This suggests that the things we see, hear, and touch are only appearances. They are only manifestations of some underlying forces, and those underlying forces are spiritual. Evidence of this is not based on study of the Bible or other ancient scriptures, but on recent discoveries of modern science.

Science is continually discovering more ways to show us that material things are not as they seem. For example, your senses may tell you that you are sitting still in a chair, but science says that you are not sitting still in that chair because of the daily rotation of the Earth. At the same time you are flying around at thousands of miles an hour because of the Earth's revolution around the sun. Further, astronomers recently have said the sun is revolving within the Milky Way galaxy, so you are flying off at a vast speed in a third direction. Even more recently astronomers have said that the Milky Way galaxy is moving away from the center of the big bang at an increasing rate of speed. So, in reality, you are flying at thousands of miles an hour in four different directions, but to you it seems as though you are sitting still.

More than a thousand books and articles have been published by natural scientists indicating that things we have always said are real are merely temporary appearances. The true reality is the spiritual background, which is the purposive cause of the material manifestation. God is permitting you to participate in the creative process. Through your thought processes you can create books and buildings and an increasing variety of objects and ideas. By influencing your thoughts God allows you to move toward the realm of the spirit.

God has given us a spectacular view of nature through science. But we must learn to look beyond, expanding our thoughts and our spirits to see the elusive but real spiritual background. Lincoln Barnett perhaps presents best the predicament of modern humankind, devoid of the vision of the Creator, at the conclusion of his book *The Universe and Dr. Einstein:*

In the evolution of scientific thought, one fact has become impressively clear: there is no mystery of the physical world which does not point to a mystery beyond itself. All high roads of the intellect, all byways of theory and conjecture lead ultimately to an abyss that human ingenuity can never span. For man is enchained by the very condition of his being, his finiteness and involvement in nature. The farther he extends his horizons, the more vividly he recognizes the fact that, as the physicist Niels Bohr puts it, "we are both spectators and actors in the great drama of existence." Man is thus his own greatest mystery. He does not understand the vast veiled universe into which he has been cast for the reason that he does not understand himself. He comprehends but little of his organic processes and even less of his unique capacity to perceive the world about him, to reason and to dream. Least of all does he understand his noblest and most mysterious faculty: the ability to transcend himself and perceive himself in the act of perception.

Man's inescapable impasse is that he himself is part of the world he seeks to explore; his body and proud brain are mosaics of the same elemental particles that compose the dark, drifting clouds of interstellar space; he is, in the final analysis, merely an ephemeral conformation of the primordial space-time field. Standing midway between macrocosm and microcosm he finds barriers on every side and can perhaps but marvel, as St. Paul did nineteen hundred years ago, that the "world was created by the word of God so that what is seen was made out of things which do not appear."[22]

For those who have opened their minds to seeing nature and reality as that which God speaks through, the words of the seventeenth-century metaphysical poet Thomas Traherne are most significant:

Your enjoyment of the world is never right till every morning you awake in Heaven; see yourself in your Father's palace; and look upon the skies, the earth, and the air as Celestial Joys: having such a reverend esteem of all, as if you were among the Angels. . . . You never enjoy the world aright . . . till your spirit filleth the whole world, and the stars are your jewels; till you are as familiar with the ways of God in all Ages as with your walk and table: till you are intimately acquainted with that shady nothing out of which the world was made; till you love men so as to desire their happiness, with a thirst equal to the zeal of your own; till you delight in God for being good at all: you never enjoy the world.[23]

NOTES

1. James M. Houston, *I Believe in the Creator* (Grand Rapids: Eerdmans, 1980), 268–69.
2. Philip Yancey, "Christian Publishing: Too Many Books and Too Few Classics?" *Christianity Today*, 2 March 1984, 21–22.
3. Arthur Peacocke, "Cosmos and Creation," in *Cosmology, History and Theology*, ed. W. Yourgran and A. D. Breck (New York: Plenum, 1977), 374.
4. Donald M. MacKay, *Science and Christian Faith Today* (London: CPAS Publications, 1960), 8–9.
5. Ibid., 9–11.
6. Lincoln Barnett, *The Universe and Dr. Einstein* (New York: Signet, 1948), 112.
7. Stanley L. Jaki, *The Road of Science and the Ways to God* (Chicago: University of Chicago Press, 1978), 192–93.
8. Ibid., 193.
9. Iain Paul, *Science, Theology and Einstein* (New York: Oxford University Press, 1982), 128.
10. Henry Drummond, *Natural Law in the Spiritual World* (1883).
11. Wil Lepkowski, "Integrating Science with Religion," *Chemical and Engineering News*, 16 January 1984, 63, 67.
12. Rustum Roy, *Experimenting with Truth* (Oxford, England: Pergamon Press, 1981).
13. Ben Shahn, *The Shape of Content* (Cambridge: Harvard University Press, 1957).
14. Pierre Teilhard de Chardin, *An Album*, ed. J. Mortier and M. Alboux (New York: Harper & Row, 1966).
15. Roy, *Experimenting with Truth*.
16. John 1:1, 3–4, KJV.
17. Vissarion Belinski, "Literary Reveries," in *The Search for God*, ed. D. M. White (New York: Macmillan, 1983).
18. John Stuart Blackie, "All Things Are Full of God," in *The Search for God*, ed. D. M. White (New York: Macmillan, 1983), 189.
19. James Jeans, *The Mysterious Universe*, rev. ed. (New York: Macmillan, 1948).
20. Henry Simmons, "Redefining the Universe," *Mosaic* 13 (March/April 1982):18.
21. Joseph Wood Krutch, *The Great Chain of Life* (New York: Pyramid, 1956), 176–77.
22. Barnett, *The Universe and Dr. Einstein*, 118–19.
23. Anne Ridley, ed., *Traherne, Poems, Centuries* (London: Oxford University Press, 1966), Centuries III, 37, 238.

3. Recent Scientific Contributions to Meaning and Purpose in the Universe

THE CURRENT SCIENTIFIC WORLDVIEW

The past few decades have witnessed scientific developments that exceed anything our imaginations could contrive. Progress in particle physics, cosmology, brain physiology, and molecular biology have combined to give us a view of a universe of staggering size and intricacy. Physicist John Polkinghorne, in his recent book, *The Way the World Is,* sums up our current understanding of cosmology as follows:

In the beginning was the big bang. The earliest moment in the history of the world that science can conceive is when the universe was concentrated into a single point. As matter expanded from this initial singularity it cooled and successive regimes decoupled from thermal equilibrium. Thus after about three minutes the temperature had dropped to a thousand million degrees. That was cool enough for deuterium to form. The arrival on the scene of this stable composite of a proton and a neutron helped to fix the global balance of hydrogen and helium in the universe for the rest of its evolution. The ratio of three to one then established is what we still observe today. After that, nothing of great significance happened for several hundred thousand years. By then the temperature had fallen sufficiently for atoms to be able to form, and this had the consequence of decoupling radiation from thermal equilibrium with the rest of the universe. That same radiation, in a form cooled by further expansion, is observable today as the universal $3°K$ background radiation discovered by Penzias and Wilson in 1965, a re-echoing whisper from those faroff times some fifteen thousand million years or so ago.

The universe continued to expand. Gravity took over and condensed matter into galaxies and the stars that compose them. In the nuclear cookery within those stars new heavy elements formed, such as carbon and iron, which had not occurred before. Dying stars, in supernova explosions, scattered these new elements into the environment. When second generation stars were formed by recondensation, their planets could be made of materials which permitted the next big development in the universe's evolution.

On at least one planet, and perhaps on millions, conditions of temperature, chemical environment, radiation, and the chance congregation of simple atoms, permitted the coming into being of quite elaborate molecules with the power of replicating themselves in that environment. In a remarkable interplay of contingent chance (to get things going) and lawful necessity (to keep them going) there had begun a process by which systems of ever-increasing complexity would evolve. On our planet this eventually led to you and me.[1]

And even though we have painted our origin with a very broad brush, recall that the cosmological parameters within which these vast transitions occur appear to be necessarily of very precise magnitude. Physicist Paul Davies, in his recent book, *Superforce,* reminds us that the existence of the complex structures of the universe seems to depend, in a very sensitive way, on the numerical values of such fundamental constants as the speed of light, the masses of the various subatomic particles, and the forces acting between these particles. These numerical values determine many of the gross features of the world: the sizes of atoms, nuclei, planets, stars, and even living things.[2]

Many of the complex structures of the universe are the result of a competition or balance between competing forces. Stars, for example, are a complexity of interplay between gravity, electromagnetic repulsion, and nuclear forces. Gravity tries to crush the stars. Electromagnetic energy resists compression by providing an internal pressure. The energy involved is released from nuclear interactions precisely as legislated by the weak and strong forces characteristic of those particles. The nature of stellar complexity therefore depends delicately on the strengths of the forces or the numerical values of the fundamental constants. Calculations show that changes in the strength of either gravity or electromagnetism by only one part in 10^{40} would spell catastrophe for stars such as the sun.

When we come to the question of life's origin, the constraints against the origination of life of any kind appear to be great. Davies comments on this:

It is sometimes objected that if the laws of physics were different, that would only mean that the structures would be different, and that while life as we know it might be impossible, some other form of life could well emerge. However, no attempt has been made to demonstrate that complex structures in general are an inevitable, or even probable, product of physical laws, and all the evidence so far indicates that many complex structures depend most delicately on the existing form of these laws. It is tempting to believe, therefore, that a complex universe will emerge only if the laws of physics are very close to what they are.[3]

Perhaps the most complex structure to emerge in the universe is humankind. But even if human beings are not that unique, we must at least recognize that the complexity of the human brain is incredible. Anatomist Gareth Jones estimates that the cerebral cortex contains 10^{10} to 10^{14} nerve cells, and that each cell contacts more than five thousand other nerve cells in precise arrangement.[4] The number of connections within one human brain rivals the number of stars in the universe!

Indeed, with the understanding that we may be the end product of this vast cosmological process comes a desire to not only understand the details of the evolution of the physical universe but also to understand the nature of ourselves as persons. What is the meaning of a universe in which the primeval assembly of fundamental particles eventually manifests the potential for organization into complex forms that are conscious and self-conscious, and that thereby transcend that matter from which they were derived? Science thus paradoxically seems to lead us, in our search for intelligibility and meaning, beyond the realm of science.

MODERN PHYSICS REVEALS AN INTELLIGIBLE TRANSCENDENT REALITY

One of the most fascinating things about the cosmos is its comprehensibility, its susceptibility to mathematical description in a way which seems to exclude the possibility of that description being simply a product of our own imagination. Polkinghorne speaks of this scientific intelligibility of the world:

Again and again in physical science we find that it is the abstract structures of pure mathematics which provide the clue to understanding the world. It is a recognized technique in fundamental physics to seek theories which have an elegant and economical (you can say beautiful) mathematical form, in the expectation that they will prove the ones realized in nature. General relativity, the modern theory of gravitation, was invented by Einstein in just such a way. Now mathematics is the free creation of the human mind, and it is surely a surprising and significant thing that a discipline apparently so unearthed should provide the key with which to turn the lock of the world.

It is this fact of intelligibility which convinces one that science is investigating the way things are. Its insights are certainly open to correction. As access is gained to new regimes, profound modifications can be called for. Thirty years ago, when I was a young research student, no one had dreamed of quarks and gluons. Who can feel confident that thirty years hence they will still be seen as the ultimate constituents of matter? Nevertheless the coherence of the inquiry into the structure of matter, the beautiful way in which the properties of previously "elementary" objects like protons and neutrons find a natural explanation in terms of their new constituents, makes one feel that it is a tale of a tightening grip on an actual reality.[5]

The reality of which Polkinghorne speaks, however, has undergone tremendous changes in the past century. From the time of Newton and even Galileo, there had been a growing conviction among scientists that reality consisted of the description of phenomena in mechanistic terms. Isaac Newton's explanation of gravitation enabled the precise calculation of the motions of the planets. The kinetic theory of gases demonstrated that atoms, too, behaved like tiny billiard balls whose pressure-volume relationships were precisely accounted for through statistical mechanics. By the end of the nineteenth century, scientists were so bold as to state that all the important basic discoveries in physics had been made. Yet within the space of a few years there occurred the discoveries of radioactivity, X rays, and the photoelectric effect, and the publication of two momentous new theories: the quantum theory and the theory of special relativity. Less than two decades later the wave nature of the electron was demonstrated. All of physical science's major concepts were brought into question, especially those that depended upon the principle of causality. This principle states that if you know the precise mechanical relationships between components before an event takes place, then the outcome of that event can be predicted with absolute certainty.

William Pollard tells us in his recent paper, "Rumors of Transcendence in Physics," that the first major confrontation of so-called natural causation was carried out by Ludwig Boltzmann, who applied the mathematics of games of chance developed for the gambling casino to physical systems in nature. Pollard explains:

This he did by equating the thermodynamic measure of the entropy of a system S to its statistical probability W through the now-famous relation $S = k \log W$. W is a measure of the number of ways in which the state of the system could be achieved and its quantitative calculation made use of formulas developed for the casino. All processes taking place naturally in the universe were irreversible and the reason why entropy always increased was that natural systems always moved to states of larger, never smaller, W. Any system in nature spontaneously moves from a less probable state to a more probable state, never the reverse, and this was taken to define the direction of the arrow of time. This was the first introduction of statistics into the description of the behavior of physical systems.

When probability is introduced anywhere in science, it means that two or more alternative responses to one and the same natural cause can be made by the system under study. Which alternative will be chosen by the system in any given instance is beyond the scope of science to specify.

The most it can do is assign probabilities to the various alternatives. As between the alternatives, science has explicitly renounced natural causation. When first introduced into science by Boltzmann, this idea was anathema to the great majority of physicists of his day and was vigorously contested. During the following three decades, however, its applications in the kinetic theory of gases, thermodynamics, and statistical mechanics convinced physicists of its validity, and Born's interpretation of quantum mechanics in terms of probability has made it a pillar of physics.[6]

Another massive shift in physical thinking was elicited by the brilliant work of Albert Einstein. Einstein's theory of special relativity was introduced in one of three papers he published during an extraordinary three-month period in 1905. Stanley Jaki tells us that any one of the three would have established Einstein's fame; the first concerned light being made up of quanta of energy, the second implicated particles of atomic size in Brownian motion, and the third, on the electrodynamics of moving bodies, later became known as the theory of special relativity.[7]

What special relativity proposes is that matter and energy are equivalent, related by the expression $E = mc^2$, where E is energy, m is the quality of inertia associated with matter, and c is the speed of light in a vacuum. Its starting point is the observed fact that the speed of light (in a vacuum) is the same for all observers no matter how they may be moving. The implications of this, in addition to the equating of mass and energy, are that nothing can be accelerated to a speed greater than that of light, and that the mass of anything increases as it approaches the velocity of light. The most startling discovery is that two events that occur at the same instant for one observer may not be simultaneous for another observer if the two are moving rapidly relative to each other. Perhaps the simplest way to summarize these various effects is to say that they blur the distinction between space and time such that they may no longer be regarded as separate entities but rather as a single whole: space-time. Here, in a single theory, we see the introduction of two revolutionary ideas: matter is actually another form of energy, and space and time are a single whole.

What kind of person was capable of such momentous thought? How did he think? What were his loyalties and liberties? What motives drove him to such earth-shaking ideas?

Perhaps it is most striking that he was a humble man who was fascinated with the universe and its Maker. In this sense he was deeply religious—profoundly moved by the mysteries of the universe, which even his great mind could scarcely comprehend. Lincoln Barnett, in his *Universe and Dr. Einstein,* quotes Einstein:

"The most beautiful and most profound emotion we can experience is the sensation of the mystical. It is the sower of all true science. He to whom this emotion is a stranger, who can no longer wonder and stand rapt in awe, is as good as dead. To know that what is impenetrable to us really exists, manifesting itself as the highest wisdom and the most radiant beauty which our dull faculties can comprehend only in their most primitive forms—this knowledge, this feeling is at the center of true religiousness."

And on another occasion he declared, "The cosmic religious experience is the strongest and noblest mainspring of scientific research."[8]

Einstein also had a deep sense of the rationality of nature that was strongly coupled with a belief in the freedom of thought and conceptualization. As Iain Paul describes it in *Science, Theology and Einstein,*

According to Einstein, scientific theories have something in common with the images of the poet. Both stimulate the intuition of the individual as resources for the apprehension of reality. Basically, any scientific theory embodies aspects of reality that are not explainable in terms of that theory. Scientific theories are not comprehensive instruction manuals. They survey empirical knowledge but necessarily with limited logic and precision. Scientific research is always returning from abroad with intimations of new continents, their differing phenomena, and the novelty of their diverse life-forms. Einstein's notion of a concept presupposes the rationality of the universe, without which it would have no vital future. On this presupposition rests the fundamental faith from which all scientific hope springs.[9]

This awareness of the reality that lies outside ourselves did not come to Einstein full-blown. Apparently he owed much to another great physicist, Max Planck.

Stanley Jaki tells us that Planck had begun his own scientific pilgrimage as a physicist against the advice of Philipp von Jolly, who held the only chair of physics at the University of Munich. Von Jolly told the seventeen-year-old Planck not to choose physics, because hardly anything more could be done there. Nevertheless, Planck studied physics at Munich and focused on thermodynamics, which appeared to him to provide a firm starting point, free of the mechanical nature of the processes themselves, because he was, in his words, "in pursuit of the ultimate, of the ever-remote goal, which consists in the presentation of all forces of nature in one single connection." It was his great success, in 1899, to describe the quantum of action, which formed the basis of quantum theory.[10]

Einstein, in the succeeding decade, had one more great contribution to make: the theory of general relativity, which was concerned with gravitation. The most important idea introduced in his general theory was that gravitation in the Newtonian sense could be replaced by a mathematical representation that involved a distortion of space-time. The existence of curved space-time means that the universe could be finite yet boundless, and with a shape like a ball. Such a universe would have a surface with no boundary, but because of the nature of curved space, it would also have no center. The realization of the existence of a finite universe has subsequently opened up the field of cosmology and has led to our present understanding of the origin of the universe in the big bang.

It was Planck who early recognized the significance of Einstein's theory of general relativity as a statement of the objective nature of the universe. As Jaki describes it,

Around 1913, when general relativity was still to be formulated in full, there was no question in Planck's mind that if a physical theory ever witnessed the absolute in the physical world, the theory of general relativity did so. Ten years after Einstein had arrived in Berlin, Planck became the first to put general relativity in that light in a widely publicized lecture, the title of which, revealingly enough, was "From the Relative to the Absolute." Planck brought his lecture to a climax with a reference to the absolute value of the metric in the four-dimensional space-time manifold. This was one of the four evidences marshaled by Planck in support of his theme. Another evidence, the absolute value of energy in terms of mass, was also of Einsteinian provenance, and Planck drew special attention to what he called the "paradox" of relativity: instead of relativizing everything, it unfolded absolute, objective aspects of the physical world.[11]

The stupendous contribution to science of this deeply religious man, Albert Einstein, and the important role of his friend Max Planck, is summed up by Jaki:

Such was the reward of traveling on a "rough and winding road," as Einstein characterized in retrospect his intellectual journey. It was a creative journey to the new science of cosmology, a science about the quantity and quantitative structure of the universe. It was a science which could only be had as a whole, as an indivisible quantum of science, or not to be had at all. Such was the deepest aspect of the identity between the two creative giants of modern physics, Planck and Einstein, and between the culminating points of their creative labors, the quantum of action and the quantity of the universe.[12]

QUANTUM MECHANICS ENDS DETERMINISM IN PHYSICS

John Polkinghorne, in his *Quantum World,* tells us that there were two great discoveries in physics in the twentieth century: special relativity and quantum mechanics.[13] Of the two, the most revolutionary was quantum mechanics, for it signaled the end of classical physics. Relativity theory, by contrast, was, in a sense, the last great flowering of the classical tradition, for it preserved the clarity of description and the thorough determinism of classical mechanics, which had been in ascendancy since the time of Newton. Indeed, Einstein had never been pleased with quantum theory, and much of his later career was spent seeking to disprove it.

Actually, it was Max Planck who laid the foundation for quantum theory, for it was he who showed that the emission and absorption of radiant energy take place in a discontinuous manner involving discrete packets, which he called quanta. The energy associated with each quantum was related to the frequency of oscillation of each particular electromagnetic radiation by the expression $E = h\upsilon$, where h is the celebrated Planck's constant.

And it was a study of Einstein's that provided one of the next important evidences of the quantized nature of radiation at the level of subatomic particles. Using Planck's quantum of action, Einstein demonstrated that the photoelectric effect, the phenomenon in which electrons were ejected from certain metals by an incident beam of light, was dependent on a critical frequency. The light was behaving like a stream of electrons, bombarding the metal surface, but it was not the intensity of the electron beam per se, but its frequency of oscillation, that determined the release of electrons. It was as though the electrons in the metal surface were like buoys anchored in a harbor. The force of the waves was somehow not the critical question in determining the breaking of the mooring lines; the frequency of the waves was. Below a certain frequency no lines were cut, regardless of the force of the waves. The concept of light energy as being made up of waves of individual particles, or photons, which collided with electrons in the metal surface, was a totally new idea.

Light thus was seen as having both wave and particle character, and physicists had to be content with the conclusion that the two models were complementary, each signifying some of the aspects of the real description of light energy. It is one of the great triumphs of quantum theory that it can embrace this apparent contradiction mathematically. In 1928 Dirac's quantum field theory succeeded in combining wave and particle nature of light without paradox.

But there were more difficult problems for physicists. It was known from the work of J. J. Thomson that there were negatively charged particles called electrons in atoms, and it was supposed that the compensating positive charge was spread out, as Polkinghorne describes it, "like the cakey part of a plum pudding, with the electrons embedded in it like currants."[14] But in 1911 Lord Rutherford demonstrated that the positive charge of the atom was instead concentrated in a pointlike object at the center of the atom, the nucleus. It was a great discovery, but it was entirely baffling for classical physics. The problem was that a planetary system of electrons rotating around a central nucleus would be unstable, because no known source could replace the loss of energy during rotation. A nuclear atomic structure was inconsistent with classical physics.

The beginning of a solution was provided by the Danish physicist Niels Bohr, who postulated that there were only certain orbits that were allowed for planetary electrons to occupy, and that these were defined by Planck's constant, h. It was noted that h was measured in the same units as those of angular momentum, a dynamic quantity that measures the amount of rotatory motion in a system. If angular momentum was quantized, or restricted to specific quantum states, then the calculations of the energy associated with each orbit fit the equations of electromagnetic radiation perfectly.

But subsequent developments placed stringent restrictions on the Bohr model, owing to the existence of what German physicist Werner Heisenberg called the uncertainty principle. Here again Planck's constant came into the picture. Heisenberg showed that there was a quantitative relationship between the position and momentum of particles of atomic dimensions, such that the product of the uncertainties in the values of these two quantities was at least of the order of magnitude of Planck's constant. This meant that Bohr's electron orbits could at best be visualized only as clouds, designating a range of possible paths, and never as discrete paths in which position and momentum would have to be simultaneously known.

Here was the end of classical physics and rigid determinism, for it was no longer possible to precisely specify the initial and final states of any process at the level of elementary particles. The philosophical significance of this situation was devastating to many scientists. In Polkinghorne's words,

This feature of quantum mechanics proved very distasteful to some of the very men who had helped to create the subject. In discussions with Bohr in September 1926, Schrodinger said "If we are going to stick to this damn quantum-jumping, then I regret that I ever had anything to do with quantum theory." Louis de Broglie also tried from time to time throughout his later life to find ways of reconciling quantum mechanics with a more deterministic picture. But the man who reacted most violently, and was never fully reconciled to this aspect of the theory, was one of its intellectual grandfathers, the great Albert Einstein, whose explanation of the photoelectric effect had been a key step in establishing the existence of the photon. In 1924 Einstein had said that if the ideas, then in the air, of renouncing strict causality proved to be correct he would "rather be a cobbler, or even an employee in a gambling house, than a physicist." Later, in a letter to Max Born, he delivered himself of his celebrated remark that he did not believe that God (whom he customarily referred to in comradely terms as "the Old One") played at dice.[15]

The specific rebuttals to quantum mechanical uncertainty have taken several forms. One group claims that the flaw is in the observer's knowledge of an event. But if we give up the reality of objective truth, originating outside ourselves, we give up science. A second group, including the Copenhagen school, suggests that the unpredictability is eliminated at the level of the classical measuring instruments of the physicist, and we therefore arrive at true knowledge. But the world of the quantum is then falsely separated from the world of the measuring instruments, yet they are depended upon to interact in some meaningful way that should be susceptible to our explanation. The third effort at explanation of uncertainty is the idea that conscious observers, rather than their measuring machines, have a special effect upon what is perceived at the microscopic level. This is different from the proposal of the first group, who simply disqualify objective knowledge. Here the external world is taken seriously as the origin of the chain of related events. But consciousness as the essential factor in the transition from microscopic uncertainty to macroscopic order is so highly anthropocentric that it raises problems of understanding physical processes prior to the advent of conscious observers.

Recall the old limerick,

> There once was a man who said, "God
> Must think it exceedingly odd
> If he finds that this tree
> Continues to be
> When there's no one about in the quad."

There is one more approach to resolving quantum mechanical uncertainty. This is the many-worlds interpretation proposed by Hugh Everett in 1957. His proposal is that where various choices are involved in the experiment each possibility is realized, but each occurs in a separate world, only one of which is that of the present observer. But each world presumably has a clone of the objects and observers, and each is unaware of the others. The biggest problem with this approach to explanation is that it multiplies entities to profusion, in violation of the principle of simplest interpretation, which we owe to William of Occam.

In any case the world of quantum mechanics has opened up vast new vistas, scientifically, philosophically, and theologically. Science as a tightly closed, self-sufficient system is gone. The possibilities for question and explanation are almost limitless.

COMPARISON OF THE SCIENTIFIC DISCIPLINES REVEALS DISTINCT LEVELS OF EXPLANATION

When we move from the explanations of our world that are provided by physical theory to the disciplines of chemistry, biology, ecology, and so on, a new set of relationships is found, a hierarchy of levels of explanation. Furthermore, there appears to be a polarity, a direction, from physics, with its most fundamental, reductionist explanation, upward to those disciplines that deal with progressively more complex components of our universe.

Arthur Peacocke, in his *Creation and the World of Science,* describes the situation as follows:

As one progresses "upwards" through the hierarchy of the sciences, for example, along the series physics-chemistry-biology-ecology or sociology, each represents a sub-class within the possible interaction of the units of the preceding level and as Medawar has noted, "the sciences become richer and richer in their empirical content and new concepts emerge at each level which simply do not appear in the preceding sciences." Corresponding to each level in the hierarchy of systems, the appropriate science employs concepts which are peculiar to it and indeed have little meaning for levels lower down (or even higher up in some cases). As new forms of matter, non-living and living, emerge in the universe, new categories of descriptions of their form and properties are necessary and these categories will be other than those of the physics and chemistry appropriate to the subnuclear, atomic, and molecular levels. Every statement which is true when applied to systems earlier (or lower) in the series is true when applied to the later (or higher), but these lower-level statements are usually not the focus of interest for the practitioners of the higher level science. Thus sociologists have insisted, recently with explosive force, on the distinctiveness of sociological concepts from biological, and biologists, for longer (and more quietly), have stressed the distinctiveness of their concepts in relation to physics and chemistry. As E. O. Wilson has put it recently, every discipline has its "antidiscipline" at the level below and is an "antidiscipline" for the level above.[16]

Peacocke goes on to provide the example of humankind as seen by the different sciences. The cosmologist sees the human as a configuration of atoms depending on the presence of certain atoms heavier than hydrogen, the basic material from which the universe was built; these heavier elements are present on the Earth as the result of high-temperature nuclear reactions and supernovae explosions occurring millions of years before the advent of our solar system. The physicist and physical chemist give an account of the structure of the atoms and the extent and rate of energy exchanges and atomic interchanges in chemical reactions going on inside the human body. The chemist provides an analysis of the composition of the elements. The biochemist describes the simpler organic molecules (eighteen vitamins, co-enzymes, and precursors; twenty-one amino acids; sixteen sugars and derivatives; four lipids and precursors; five purines, pyrimidines, and derivatives; and nine other molecules) and the metabolic pathways whereby they are interconnected in the human body. The molecular biologist relates this system of components to the macromolecular architecture of the cells, including the genetic machinery involving DNA, messenger RNA, and protein synthesis. The biologist builds these components into cell systems, differentiated tissues, and the structures unique to the human. The physiologist interrelates these functional structures or organs to the biochemical components involved in their regulation and function. The neurophysiologist focuses on that enormously complicated organ, the brain. In the human this organ contains 10^{10} long nerve cells, each of which makes contact with ten thousand other cells through special interfaces under control of chemical messengers.

Even the brain of a rat far exceeds in complexity any human artifact, a complexity wonderfully described in Sir Charles Sherrington's famous description of the waking brain as an "enchanted loom where millions of flashing shuttles weave a dissolving pattern, always a meaningful pattern though never an abiding one; a shifting harmony of sub-patterns."

Finally, Peacocke reminds us, there are distinct levels of scientific description, such as ethology, concerning animal behavior, and ecology, concerning the geographical distribution and adaptation of populations, that are relevant to humankind.

The distinction between levels of description is extremely important in order to avoid the error of attempting to reduce everything to chemistry and physics, a favorite goal of some zealous basic scientists. The fallacy of this approach is addressed by Donald MacKay in *The Clockwork Image:*

In order to avoid confusion we must note that the term "reductionism" is sometimes used for the well-established scientific habit of taking things to bits in order to understand them. Thus chemists seek to understand the behaviour of molecules by analysing them into atomic nuclei and electrons. Biologists seek to understand cell membranes by analysing them into molecules; and so on. . . . In biology, . . . it becomes dangerous only if the scientist imagines that *all* questions of biological interest can be stated and handled in the terms of chemistry or of physics. For the truth is that physics and chemistry have no terms for some of the main concepts and problems that interest the biologist.

What are the chemical or physical equivalents of biological "adaptation," for example? At first sight the answer might seem simple. The chemist or physicist would expect (in principle) to be able to explain what all the atoms and molecules are doing in an animal that is or becomes well adapted to its environment. But does that make "adaptation" a physical concept? Of course not; indeed for physics as such it is strictly meaningless. It is defined for an approach from a different angle, so to speak, an approach which in no way denies the validity of the other, but which recognizes aspects that the other misses. If the biologist were compelled to talk only at the level of physics he would be unable even to *pose* his most characteristic problems, let alone to solve them.

It has sometimes been suggested that the difficulty should be resolved by simply adding such biological terms to the dictionary of physics; but this suggestion misses the point. At the risk of labouring the obvious, let us spell out why. It is not that physics lacks a *word* for adaptation: the point is that, given the approach of physics, the *concept* cannot be defined. Physics is our name for a particular way of taking a situation to bits; and once you have reduced a situation to the "bits" of physics, you no longer have the "whole" to which the biologist points when he uses such terms as adaptation.[17]

Scientific explanation, especially of living systems, thus involves a more complex process of description than we had thought heretofore. Biological systems seem not to be reducible to physicochemical explanation, not because of some vitalism they exhibit, but rather because the methodologies of physics and biology are fundamentally different.

This new understanding of the nature of complex scientific descriptions of systems is of considerable significance. It helps us to avoid the trap of assuming exclusive and complete explanations in any one scientific discipline. The result of that exclusivist kind of thinking can be the elevation of physicochemical explanation to the status of ultimate truth, as though other explanations, whether from the so-called soft sciences, such as human biology or psychology, or from theology or the humanities, were of no value. A proper understanding of levels of explanation also enables us to study more effectively the relationships in such fields as evolutionary theory, which are often a composite of several complex systems traversing multiple levels of explanation. It also holds out the possibility that there may be still other levels of explanation, beyond those of human behavior and neurophysiology, that await our study. Clearly the dependence of higher levels on lower levels of description suggests a wholeness of relationships, and the existence of new aspects and concepts in each successive higher level implies that future levels of scientific explanation will reveal new and astounding aspects of humankind and its Creator. The future gives promise that the enormous and intricate tapestry that is our scientific understanding of the creation will become more and more evident.

PROCESSES DEPEND UPON THE INTERPLAY OF CHANCE AND NECESSITY

Recalling the vast sweep of processes leading to intelligent life that were briefly described at the beginning of this chapter, the fine structure of their interactions, the explanation for their direction, and their remarkable result seem best understood in terms of some special type of interplay between chance and necessity. As Polkinghorne expresses it,

The processes of the world seem to depend for their fruitfulness upon an interplay between chance and necessity. A random event (an aggregation of atoms, a genetic mutation) produces a new possibility which is then given a perpetuating stability by the regularity of the laws of nature. Without contingent chance, new things would not happen. Without lawful necessity to preserve them in an environment whose reliability permits competitive selection, they would vanish away as soon as they were made. The universe is full of the clatter of monkeys playing with typewriters, but once they have hit on the first line of *Hamlet* it seems that they are marvellously constrained to continue to the end of at least some sort of play.

To many, this apparent role of chance is a sign of the emptiness and pointlessness of the world. In his book *Chance and Necessity* Jacques Monod wrote, "pure chance, absolutely free but blind, [is] at the very root of the stupendous edifice of evolution," and he concluded his book by writing,

The ancient covenant is in pieces; man at last knows that he is alone in the unfeeling vastness of the universe, out of which he emerged by chance. Neither his destiny nor his duty have been written down.

When I read Monod's book I was greatly excited by the scientific picture it presented of how life came to be. As a particle physicist, I found the biochemical details pretty difficult to follow but, assuming them to be correct, they implied that Schrodinger's equation and Maxwell's equations (the fundamental dynamical equations of quantum theory and electromagnetism respectively, which I could literally write down on the back of an envelope) had this astonishing consequence of the emergence of replicating molecules and eventually life. The economy and profundity of that is breathtaking. For me, the beauty that it revealed in the structure of the world was like a rehabilitation of the argument from design—not as a knockdown argument for the existence of God (there are no such arguments; nor are there for his non-existence) but as an insight into the way the world is.[18]

There have been many other rebuttals to Monod's atheistic conclusions. This is the response of Arthur Peacocke:

I see no reason why this randomness of molecular event in relation to biological consequence, that Monod rightly emphasizes, has to be raised to the level of a metaphysical principle interpreting the universe. . . . In the behaviour of matter on a larger scale many regularities, which have been raised to the level of being describable as "laws," arise from the combined effect of random microscopic events which constitute the macroscopic. So the involvement of chance at the level of mutations does not, of itself, preclude these events manifesting a law-like behaviour at the level of populations of organisms and indeed of populations of biosystems that may be presumed to exist on the many planets throughout the universe which might support life. Instead of being daunted by the role of chance in genetic mutations as being the manifestation of irrationality in the universe, it would be more consistent with the observations to assert that the full gamut of the potentialities of living matter could be explored only through the agency of the rapid and frequent randomization which is possible at the molecular level of the DNA. In other words, the designation "chance" in this context refers to the multiple effects whereby the (very large) number of mutations are elicited that constitute the "noise" which, via an independent causal chain, the environment then selects for viability. This role of chance is what one would expect if the universe were so constituted as to be able to explore all the potential forms of organizations of matter (both living and non-living) which it contains. Moreover, even if the present biological world *is* only one out of an already large number of possibilities, it must be the case that the potentiality of forming such a world is present in the fundamental constitution of matter as it exists in our universe. The original primeval cloud of fundamental particles must have had the potentiality of being able to develop into the complex molecular forms we call modern biological life. . . . I see no reason why God should not allow the potentialities of his universe to be developed in all their ramifications through the operation of random events; indeed, in principle, this is the only way in which all potentialities might eventually, given enough time and space, be actualized.[19]

But there is here a certain detachment of God from his creation, which somehow seems inconsistent with the biblical notions of providence and chance. William Pollard, in his *Chance and Providence,* seeks to retain an immanent Creator in the seemingly random processes themselves. To Einstein's famous question, "Does God throw dice?" he says the Judeo-Christian answer is not, as so many have wrongly supposed, a denial, but a very positive affirmative.[20]

For Pollard, God is working intimately in the complexity of relationships, which he describes as a maze, a fabric of turning points, open at every step to new choices and new direction. Here, God is not altering the natural probabilities but rather selecting from all the alternatives at each turning point.

EVOLUTION AS INTERPLAY OF CHANCE AND NECESSITY

The many and varied ancient ideas of the world had certain things in common: constricted dimensions, a mechanistic structure, and a static character.

As for their constricted dimensions, even in the Ptolemaic picture of things, which continued in vogue for more than a thousand years, the Earth was seen as a globe encompassed by huge crystalline spheres. It was not until our own time that people became aware of the gigantic dimensions and amazing structure of the universe. By this we mean that people used to see the world as a combination of heterogeneous elements that were in some way put together extraneously and had only a mechanical link with one another. A view of this sort made no proper allowance for the reciprocal cohesion of all entities. Just as a machine is made up of a number of previously prepared components, so people imagined the world to be a huge mechanism in which a variety of preconstituted and mutually independent entities had been artificially conjoined. The Earth, the vault of heaven, plants, animals, and humankind were thus envisaged as so many diverse "creatures," subsisting independently of each other, and made up into a whole only in the way that the pieces of furniture in a living room are. In the modern world-picture there is a complete reversal of these conditions. Science has gradually made it more clear that all entities are continuously and intrinsically interconnected, so that we can now see the world as a mighty organic whole in which every single thing is related to everything else. The world in which we live presents itself to us not as a machine, artificially contrived, but as an organism building itself up from within; an organism in which all entities have appeared through a stage-by-stage process of growth.

Finally, the old world-picture stood for the firm belief that the universe was to be conceived of as a fundamentally changeless and static whole. Of course people were not blind to the mutations and motions occurring in the world; but as they saw it, these changes were always on the surface of things and did not affect their essential nature. From its moment of origin, everything assumed a form and aspect that was definitive and unchanging. The machine worked, it was activated; but the machine itself never altered. Along with the mechanistic view of the world, the static view of it has also disintegrated. Nowadays we see the universe as an enormous historical process, an evolutionary happening that has been going on for thousands of millions of years and is moving on into an incalculable future.

The concept of chance, of a probabilistic way of looking at events and processes came on the scientific scene at about the time that Charles Darwin proposed his theory of organic evolution. It entered the static, mechanistic world of Isaac Newton, a world of cause and effect, and brought about a profound change—scientifically, philosophically, and theologically—in the way we perceive the world. C. H. Waddington, in his *Nature of Life,* tells us that the idea of evolution was not entirely new, having been anticipated by the ancient Greeks, and appreciated even by St. Thomas Aquinas and St. Augustine in the Middle Ages.[21] But what Darwin brought with his theory of organic evolution was the novel idea of the production of new genotypes, of recombination and fertilization, as random chance events. The subsequent impact of Darwin's theory, and especially the notion of chance, on theological thinking, is described by Waddington as follows:

This emphasis on the importance of chance has been one of the most profound and far-reaching of Darwin's influences on human thought. It spread into fields far removed from those which Darwin discussed. As we all know, during this century there has been a strong tendency to frame the laws of physics in terms of probability or chance events, rather than in terms of the type of simple causation which had been relied on by Newton.

Within the field of evolution the rival type of hypothesis, which the reliance on chance superseded, was one which depended on the operations of an intelligent designer. Darwin himself, to some extent at least, shared the feelings of many of his contemporaries, that the substitution of chance for design as an explanatory principle tended to undermine one of the major intellectual reasons for a belief in God. "I may say," he wrote in one of his letters, "that the impossibility of conceiving that this grand and wondrous universe, with our conscious selves, arose through chance, seems to me the chief argument for the existence of God; but whether this is an argument of real value, I have never been able to decide. . . . The safest conclusion seems to be that the whole subject is beyond the scope of man's intellect. . . ."

Many of his readers, particularly those who were not scientists, could not bring themselves to adopt such a neutral attitude, and felt deeply shocked. As Irvine has put it, "Darwin's explanation of evolution is mechanistic without the favourable implications of mechanical design. Natural selection represents not a harmony but a conflict, and is effected not by the precise, mathematical idealism of invisible force, but apparently by a crude, random sorting out of variations by the environment. . . . Many who were willing to believe in an evolving Deity could not believe in one who dealt in random variations. They could accept an evolving universe but not a universe shaken out of a dice box."[22]

We have already addressed the way in which random chance events may be perceived as the Creator's activity, but we should also consider the fact that there is another meaning for the word *chance*, which lends further insight into the way we may see God's hand in the interplay of chance and necessity. Donald MacKay, in *Clockwork Image*, distinguishes two kinds of chance. In the scientific sense chance is often used as a technical term indicating the absence of the knowledge of causal connections between events. In popular usage, however, chance signifies instead a mindless chaos, the so-called blind chance, and it is this metaphysical notion that Darwin saw as an alternative to God.[23]

MacKay points out that during the nineteenth-century debates on the role of chance in biology, the two uses of the word *chance* became confused, so that science seemed to be making unjustifiable metaphysical assertions, and the Bible got the reputation of denying the validity of the purely technical, and theologically neutral, scientific notion of chance. As usual, the Bible itself has clues that ought to have warned us against this. Chance is mentioned in the sense of chaos in Genesis 1:2, where the Earth is described as "without form and void," but here it is only as something banished from the world by God's creative word. Chance in the neutral scientific sense, however, is mentioned as a part of God's plan. "The lot is cast into the lap," says Proverbs 16:33, "but the decision is wholly from the Lord." Here is a clear indication that God is the Lord of events, which in this sense happen by chance, just as much as he is Lord of those that seem orderly to us. It may be easier for us to see God's hand in the obviously orderly pattern; but the Bible seems to exclude the idea that he must always work in this way. The either/or notion (either God or chance) is simply not the way the Bible relates the two, if we take *chance* in the first, technical sense.

Clearly, from what was said earlier, there is also the occasional use of the term *chance* in its random sense, as though it were a scientific term. But even here concerns have been expressed that the random component is overemphasized, because there appear to be ordering and structuring forces involved in the evolutionary mechanism in close proximity to the initiating events in mutation.

For example, Gordon Taylor, in his *Great Evolution Mystery,* discusses the possibility of an inherent self-stabilization of the genome as an important selective factor in evolution. He mentions L. L. Whyte's proposal, in *Internal Factors in Evolution,* that the genome is self-stabilizing; it will accept only mutations that increase, or at least are neutral with respect to, its stability. In other words, only those mutations that satisfy certain stringent physical, chemical, and functional conditions can survive the complex chromosomal, nuclear, and cellular activities involved in the processes of cell division, growth, and function. The number of possible variations is seen as limited. Perhaps the genome can modify nearly acceptable mutations. Probably it can handle groups of mutations, each of which alone might be unacceptable, if the overall effect is stabilizing. Taylor points out that if Whyte is right, no mutation is due entirely to chance: only those that meet the internal demands of the genome can be utilized in evolutionary processes.[24]

Equally intriguing is the existence of so-called dissipative structures, a class of steady-state systems that occurs in certain far-from-equilibrium situations, which is implicated by Nobel laureate Ilya Prigogine in the ordering process in evolution. It is granted that the increase in order and complexity in the evolution of living things is explainable thermodynamically as occurring at the expense of the free energy of compounds, which are broken down for energy, and by the return of heat to the environment. But there remain serious questions as to the large changes that have occurred in the course of evolution, not only in the origin of the first cell-like structure, but also in numerous large jumps, or emergences, within the subsequent evolutionary sequence. Nonequilibrium thermodynamics seems to be a likely agency in these bold transitions.

Arthur Peacocke addresses this development:

We know that, in systems near to equilibrium, any fluctuations away from that state will be damped down and the system will tend to revert to its equilibrium state. What Prigogine and his colleagues have been able to show is that there exists a class of steady-state systems, "dissipative structures," which by taking in matter and energy can maintain themselves in an ordered, steady state far from equilibrium. In such states there can occur, under the right conditions, fluctuations which are no longer damped and which are amplified so that the system changes its whole structure to a *new* ordered state in which it can again become steady and imbibe energy and matter from the outside and maintain its new structured form. This instability of dissipative structures has been studied by these workers who have set out more precisely the thermodynamic conditions for a dissipative structure to move from one state to a new state which is more ordered than previously. It turns out that these conditions are not so restrictive that no systems can ever possibly obey them. Indeed a very large number of systems, such as those of the first living forms of matter which must have involved complex networks of chemical reactions, are very likely to do so, since they are non-linear in the relationship between the forces and fluxes involved (which is one of the necessary conditions for these fluctuations to be amplified).[25]

In Prigogine's own words,

We . . . begin to understand, in quantitative terms, the role of the statistical element in the description of a [dissipative] system . . . we are led to a first parallelism between dissipative structure formation and certain features occurring in the early stages of biogenesis and the subsequent evolution to higher forms. The analogy would even become closer if the model we discuss has further critical points of unstable transition. One would then obtain a hierarchy of dissipative structures, each one enriched further by the information content of the previous models through the "memory" of the initial fluctuations which created them successively.[26]

Manfred Eigen and his coworkers have also addressed the problem of the origin of living systems, building on a now widely accepted hypothesis that the replicating macromolecules of the simple, precellular systems underwent an evolutionlike process. Synthesis occurred by interaction of smaller components, to yield macromolecular structures by the ordinary physicochemical laws of molecular interaction. But once a group or family of these macromolecules had formed, a random selection process would search out from all the various structures that small number that had utility for the developing system—catalytic activity, stabilization, or whatever—and thereby generate a kind of dominant species. The key to the success of the process is in the balance of deterministic and random events, the former ensuring that useful macromolecular species will survive, the latter providing the capacity for creative experimentation within existing structures. Here again the random component appears to be anything but blind. Instead it appears peculiarly well situated to achieve a very purposeful end.[27]

The work of Prigogine and Eigen and their collaborators demonstrates the subtlety of the interplay of apparent randomness and determinism in the processes that appear to have led to the emergence of living things. This interplay, according to Peacocke, is of such a creative character as to make it

inevitable both that living structures should emerge and that they should evolve—given the physical and chemical properties of the atomic units (and presumably, therefore, of sub-atomic particles) in the universe we

actually have. One obtains the impression that the universe has potentialities which are becoming actualized by the joint operation, in time, of
chance and law, of random time-dependent processes in a framework of
law-like determined properties—and that these potentialities include the
possibility of biological, and so of human, life.[28]

What seems increasingly evident is that our enormous universe
is nevertheless finite, intelligible, and purposeful. At each successive level of its complexity, new potentialities are realized, and
new concepts and methods are applicable. To the extent that we
can talk of random chance events in the evolution of our cosmos,
they seem remarkably constrained to yield some useful and often
astonishing products.

All of this is consistent with the existence of a transcendent God
of infinite wisdom who evidences intimate concern for his creatures yet encourages the operation of free will in his Creation.

These are the conclusions, too, of an increasing body of scientists in our day. Physicist Paul Davies, at the conclusion of his
most recent book, *Superforce,* asks,

Should we conclude that the universe is a product of design? The new
physics and the new cosmology hold out a tantalizing promise: that we
might be able to explain how all the physical structures in the universe
have come to exist, automatically, as a result of natural processes. We
should then no longer have need for a Creator in the traditional sense.
Nevertheless, though science may explain the world, we still have to
explain science. The laws which enable the universe to come into being
spontaneously seem themselves to be the product of exceedingly inge-
nious design. If physics is the product of design, the universe must have
a purpose, and the evidence of modern physics suggests strongly to me
that the purpose includes us.[29]

NOTES

1. John Polkinghorne, *The Way the World Is* (Grand Rapids: Eerdmans, 1983), 7.
2. Paul Davies, *Superforce* (New York: Simon and Schuster, 1984), 242.
3. Davies, *Superforce,* 243.
4. Gareth Jones, *Our Fragile Brains* (Downers Grove, IL: InterVarsity Press, 1980),
   38–39.
5. Polkinghorne, *The Way the World Is,* 9.

6. William Pollard, "Rumors of Transcendence in Physics," *American Journal of Physics* 52 (1984): 877–81.
7. Stanley L. Jaki, *The Road of Science and the Ways to God* (Chicago: University of Chicago Press, 1978), 181.
8. Lincoln Barnett, *The Universe and Dr. Einstein* (New York: Signet, 1948), 118.
9. Iain Paul, *Science, Theology and Einstein* (New York: Oxford University Press, 1982), 35–36.
10. Jaki, *Road of Science and the Ways to God*, 168–69.
11. Jaki, *Road of Science*, 183.
12. Jaki, *Road of Science*, 190.
13. John Polkinghorne, *The Quantum World* (London: Longmans, 1984), ix.
14. Polkinghorne, *The Quantum World*, 9.
15. Polkinghorne, *The Quantum World*, 53–54.
16. Arthur R. Peacocke, *Creation and the World of Science* (Oxford: Clarendon Press, 1979), 116–17.
17. Donald M. MacKay, *The Clockwork Image* (Downers Grove, IL.: InterVarsity Press, 1974), 44–45.
18. Polkinghorne, *The Quantum World*, 11–12.
19. Peacocke, *Creation and the World of Science*, 94–95.
20. William G. Pollard, *Chance and Providence* (London: Faber, 1958), 97.
21. C. H. Waddington, *The Nature of Life* (New York: Atheneum, 1962), 73–77.
22. Waddington, *The Nature of Life*, 85–86.
23. MacKay, *The Clockwork Image*, 49.
24. Gordon R. Taylor, *The Great Evolution Mystery* (New York: Harper & Row, 1983), 239–40.
25. Peacocke, *Creation and the World of Science*, 98–99.
26. Ilya Prigogine and G. Nicolis, *Quant. Rev. Biophysics* 4 (1971): 132.
27. Manfred Eigen, *Naturwissenschaften* 58 (1971): 465.
28. Peacocke, *Creation and the World of Science*, 103–104.
29. Davies, *Superforce*, 243.

4. God Reveals Himself in the Astronomical and in the Infinitesimal

MODERN COSMOGONY APPEARS TO PARALLEL BIBLICAL COSMOGONY

The notion of design, the tracing of the superintelligent ordering of the universe, was foundational to the writers of Scripture. Thus St. Paul wrote,

For since the creation of the world, God's invisible qualities—his eternal power and divine nature—have been clearly seen being understood from what has been made.[1]

The awesome world we survey with our eyes and ears and sift through our hands has been sensed by poet and philosopher alike. Elizabeth Barrett Browning captures it best when she writes,

> Earth's crammed with Heaven,
> And Every common bush afire with God;
> But only he who sees takes off his shoes.
> The rest sit round it and pluck blackberries.[2]

It is, too, the special domain of astrophysicist and astronomer, some of whom, such as Owen Gingerich at Harvard, see God's hand, and others, such as Carl Sagan, choose to think of themselves as being a bit like Prometheus, stealing fire from the gods.

Some of the "fire" in Sagan's writing is seen in this passage from *Cosmos:*

The surface of the Earth is the shore of the cosmic ocean. From it we have learned most of what we know. Recently, we have waded a little out to sea, enough to dampen our toes, or, at most, wet our ankles. The water seems inviting. The ocean calls. Some part of our being knows this is from where we came. We long to return. These aspirations are not, I think, irreverent, although they may trouble whatever gods may be.[3]

Contrary to Sagan's feelings, there are many in science today who find the exploration of space and the study of the life it bears a positive act of reverence for the Designer. Harvard astrophysicist Owen Gingerich catches the essence of the beginning when he says in his Dwight lecture of 1982,

During this past decade, knowledge of the world of the smallest possible sizes, the domain of particle physics, has been combined with astronomy to describe the universe in its opening stages. The physics ultimately fails as the nucleo-cosmologists push their calculations back to Time Zero, but they get pretty close to the beginning, to 10^{-43} second. At that point, at a second split so fine that no clock could measure it, the entire observable universe is compressed within the wavelike blur described by the uncertainty principle, so tiny and compact that it could pass through the eye of a needle. Not just this room, or the earth, or the solar system, but *the entire universe* squeezed into a dense dot of pure energy. And then comes the explosion. "There is no way to express that explosion" writes the poet Robinson Jeffers.

> *". . . All that exists*
> *Roars into flame, the tortured fragments rush away*
> *from each other into all the sky, new universes*
> *Jewel the black breast of night; and far off the*
> *outer nebulae like charging spearmen again*
> *Invade emptiness."*

It is an amazing picture, of pure and incredibly energetic light being transformed into matter, and leaving its vestiges behind—countless atoms and even more numerous photons of light generated in that mighty blast. . . .

This is indeed a thrilling scenario, of all that exists roaring into flame and charging forth into emptiness. And its essential framework, of everything springing forth from that blinding flash, bears a striking resonance with those succinct words of Genesis 1:3: "And God said, Let there be light." Who could have guessed even a hundred years ago, not to mention two or three thousand years ago, that a scientific picture would emerge with electro-magnetic radiation as the starting point of creation! According to the NASA astrophysicist Robert Jastrow, the agnostic scientists should sit up and take notice, and even be a little worried. But let us look a little more carefully at the extent of the convergence. Both the contemporary scientific account and the age old Biblical account assume a beginning. The scientific account concerns only the transformation of everything that now is. It does not go beyond that, to the singularity when there was nothing and then suddenly the inconceivably energetic seed for the universe abruptly came into being. Here science seems up against a blank wall. In one memorable passage in his book, *God and the Astronomers,* Jastrow says: "At this moment it seems as though science will never be able to raise the curtain on the mystery of creation. For the scientist who has lived by his faith in the power of reason, the story ends like a bad dream. He has scaled the mountains of ignorance; he is about to conquer the highest peak; as he pulls himself over the final rock, he is greeted by a band of theologians who have been sitting there for centuries."[4]

It is tempting to add to Jastrow's story. Think of the excitement as our scientist climber explains his interpretation of the biblical statement, "Let there be light" to the theologians. How much he has added! How stupendous the light-giving becomes when read out in astrophysical terms!

Yet the mysteries of the cosmos are not restricted to that first cataclysmic moment. Similar feelings of awe and perplexity are expressed by biologists who have studied mechanisms for the origin of life. Just what sequence of events could have led by physicochemical means to the advent of the first primitive cell? The improbabilities seem unsurmountable without the intervention of the Designer, without the correct ordering of reactions and environmental factors exploiting the inherent propensities of the stuff of life. It would seem more and more difficult to accept the opening phrase of Sagan's *Cosmos:* "The Cosmos is all that is or ever was or ever will be."[5] You may choose to make God in your own image, but the data of science give you no solace in that lonely choice. It would seem instead that the known cosmos is only the beginning of a revelation of the size of God! Indeed, that band of theologians on the mountaintop have just begun their work.

But perhaps the most powerful recent source of support for design in the universe builds upon what has been called the anthropic principle.[6] This principle, first described by Robert Dicke of Princeton in 1961, takes notice of the fact that this vast assemblage of cosmological evidence describes a universe that is peculiarly suited for the production of life. Dicke had been analyzing work done by P. A. M. Dirac in the 1930s, in which he observed a curious numerical relationship between some so-called dimensionless numbers, which are fundamental measures of force, time, and mass. Dirac found a numerical value of 10^{-40} for the coupling strength of gravitational force, a value of 10^{40} for the age of the universe, and a value of 10^{80} for the mass of the universe; he noted that they differed from each other by the integral power of 10^{40}. He proposed that the phenomenon was a manifestation of some unknown causal connection, a conclusion that satisfied most physicists, who then moved on to better things. But not Robert Dicke, who sought to explain the coincidence of these seemingly unrelated numbers. He suggested that the order of magnitude relationship between gravitational force and the mass of the universe could be explained on the basis of an effect of gravitational force of distant matter on the inertial mass of individual particles of the universe. But this relationship, if valid, would be true in all eras of the history of the universe. What, then, was the relationship of these two parameters to the age of the universe? Dicke's conclusion was that the numerical value for the age of the universe is strongly constrained by the conditions necessary for the existence of humankind. That is, in an evolutionary universe originating in a big bang, its age is not permitted to take one of an enormous range of values. Instead, it is limited by the biological requirements to be met for the appearance of humankind. For our evolution to proceed, there must be raw materials in the form of the elements carbon, oxygen, and nitrogen, of which we are composed, yet the cosmologists describe the original fireball as containing only the lightest elements: hydrogen, helium, and a little lithium. To go beyond this point, to set the stage for the advent of intelligent life, stars must be formed and then decayed in the form of supernovae, in order to generate the heavier elements. And those elements must in turn be incorporated into a planet of a small star, our sun, whose longevity is approximately five billion years and whose thermal characteristics assure us of moderate temperatures and the possibility of several billion more years of life before evolving into a red giant and finally engulfing our planet. Cosmologists can assign a minimum time for this evolutionary stage-setting for the advent of intelligent life on Earth, and it is this figure that appears to correlate with the age of the universe and hence with the other cosmological parameters of force and mass.

Another way of describing the phenomenon is to say that the age of an *inhabited* universe cannot be shorter than the age of the shortest-lived star, because the heavier elements of which we are made depend for their formation upon the conversion of a large, short-lived star into a supernova.

DESIGN IN THE UNIVERSE

The most intriguing part of the picture is the way in which each of the cosmological parameters is delicately poised, so that a slight change would radically alter the nature of the cosmos, perhaps even excluding the possibility of intelligent life. For example, as Henry Simmons describes it in the March/April 1982 issue of *Mosaic,* a slight increase in the gravitational force would make all stars blue giants, producing heavier elements through supernova formation but having a lifetime of only a few tens of millions of years, too brief for the appearance of intelligent life. If the gravitational force were slightly smaller, all stars would be hydrogen-burning dwarfs like our sun. Their lifetimes would be tens of billions of years, ample for the evolution of intelligent life, but there would be no source of the heavier elements essential for life as we know it. Recall Simmons's conclusion, of Chapter 2:

Thus the value of the gravitational coupling seems precisely poised to permit the evolution of a particular universe. This universe must contain

short-lived, metal-scattering, blue-giant stars; long-lived, evenly burning, slowly turning stars such as the sun; and observers.[7]

The same delicate balance is seen in other fundamental physical
constants of our universe. The strong force that holds the atomic
nucleus together, compensating for the powerful repulsion of the
like-charged protons, is necessary for the formation of the heavier
elements. A slight weakening and the universe would consist only
of hydrogen. Equally narrow limits of variation are essential for
electromagnetic force, for the ratio of the masses of the electron
and proton, and for the weak force mediating interatomic binding.
Dicke has also remarked on the crucial nature of the rate of expansion of the universe, as follows:

If the rate of expansion in the early universe were only one part in 10^{14}
smaller, the universe would have recollapsed before it would have formed
stars and galaxies. And if this expansion rate were increased very slightly,
by only one part in 10^{14}, the universe would expand too rapidly to permit
density fluctuations in the early universe to condense into bound systems
like galaxies.[8]

It is not difficult to see, in this remarkable ordering of the universe, the hand of a Designer, guiding within narrow limits the
direction, magnitude, and timing of each event of the universe,
from that staggering explosion billions of years ago to the present.
Indeed, as we come closer to the present, to the period of life's
origin, we encounter again a remarkable confluence of essential
conditions.

Owen Gingerich, in his Dwight lecture of 1982, comments su-
perbly on the marvelous way in which the data of science seems
to form a beautiful panoramic tapestry of grand design. Among
the many "vestiges of the designer's hand" to be seen, he chooses
to speak about the remarkable relationship between the atmosphere of our Earth and the appearance of life.

From what astronomers have deduced about solar evolution, we believe
that the sun was perhaps 25% less luminous several billion years ago.
Today, if the solar luminosity dropped by 25%, the oceans would freeze

solid to the bottom, and it would take a substantial increase beyond the sun's present luminosity to thaw them out again. Life could not have originated on such a frozen globe, so it seems that the earth's surface never suffered such frigid conditions. As it turns out, there is a very good reason for this. The original atmosphere would surely have consisted of hydrogen, by far the most abundant element in the universe, but this light element would have rapidly escaped, and a secondary atmosphere of carbon dioxide and water vapor would have formed from the outgassing of volcanoes. This secondary atmosphere would have produced a strong greenhouse effect, an effect that might be more readily explained with a locked car parked in the sun on a hot summer day than with a greenhouse. When you open the car, it's like an oven inside. The glass lets in the photons of visible light from the sun. Hot as the interior of the car may seem, it's quite cool compared to the sun's surface, so the reradiation from inside the car is in the infrared. The glass is quite opaque for those longer wavelengths, and because the radiation can't get out, the car heats up inside. Similarly, the carbon dioxide and water vapor partially blocked the reradiation from the early earth, raising its surface temperature above the mean freezing point of water.

As the sun's luminosity rose over the ages, so did the surface temperature of the earth, and had the atmosphere stayed constant, our planet would now have a runaway greenhouse effect, something like that found on the planet Venus; the earth's oceans would have boiled away, leaving a hot, lifeless globe.

How did our atmosphere change over to oxygen just in the nick of time? Apparently the earliest widely successful life forms on earth were the so-called blue-greens, a single-celled prokaryote, which survive to this day as stromatolites. Evidence for them appears in the Precambrian fossil record of a billion years ago. In the absence of predators, these algae-like organisms covered the oceans, extracting hydrogen from the water and releasing oxygen to the air. Nothing much seems to have happened for over a billion years, which is an interesting counterargument to those who claim intelligent life is the inevitable result whenever life forms. However, about 600 million years ago the oxygen content of the atmosphere rose rapidly, and then a series of events, quite possibly interrelated, took place: 1) eukaryotic cells, that is, cells with their genetic information contained within a nucleus, originated which allowed the invention of sex and the more efficient sharing of genetic material, and hence a more rapid adaptation of life forms to new environments; 2) more complicated organisms breathing oxygen, with its much higher energy yield, developed; and 3) the excess carbon dioxide was converted into limestone in the structure of these creatures, thus making the atmosphere more transparent in the infrared and thereby preventing the oceans from boiling away in a runaway greenhouse effect as the sun brightened. The perfect timing of this complex configuration of circumstances is enough to amaze and bewilder many of my friends who look at all this in purely mechanistic terms—the survival of life on earth seems such a close shave as to border on the miraculous.[9]

THE UNIQUENESS OF OUR BIOSPHERE

Life seems not only tenuous, but also rare. As we venture out onto the cosmic sea, we are impressed with how much of it is apparently empty space, devoid of matter and so also devoid of life as we know it. Sagan describes our predicament gloomily when he writes,

The Earth is a place. It is by no means the only place. It is not even a typical place. No planet or star or galaxy can be typical, because the Cosmos is mostly empty. The only typical place is within the vast, cold, universal vacuum, the everlasting night of intergalactic space, a place so strange and desolate that, by comparison, planets and stars and galaxies seem achingly rare and lovely. If we were randomly inserted into the Cosmos, the chance that we would find ourselves on or near a planet would be less than one in a billion trillion (10^{33}, a one followed by 33 zeroes). In everyday life such odds are called compelling. Worlds are precious.[10]

And even where there are relatively near neighbors, as in our own solar system, such neighbors seem alien and forbidding to us in our search for life. Picture yourself on a spacecraft, *Voyager 2*, launched from Cape Canaveral in July 1979. Actually, despite the fact that the satellite is the size of an average living room, it is so full of equipment for power generation and space measurements that you and I really can't squeeze aboard. But let's imagine!

On the thirteenth day of our voyage, we accomplish a "space first," photographing the Earth and moon together. At day 150 we fire rocket engines briefly for a slight correction of our spiral course. At day 215 we cross the orbit of Mars, our nearest planetary neighbor on this voyage to the outer planets. Mars had shown early promise as another place for life to develop, but the various satellites that have visited it have turned up no evidence of life forms of any kind. Despite astronomer Percival Lowell's lifelong expectations, based primarily on the so-called Martian canals and H. G. Wells's *War of the Worlds,* there are no living creatures on the cold, sandy, and boulder-strewn planet. And, it might be added, looking back over our shoulders far behind us and much nearer the sun, the planet Venus is also a totally unlikely place for life: hot, dry, and without an atmosphere.

On day 295 we begin a perilous six-month journey through a large band of asteroids—massive, tumbling boulders sailing by us ominously. Another three months beyond the asteroid belt, we begin to see the massive planet Jupiter clearly, more clearly than with any telescope on Earth. It is immense, a swirling mass of dense gases and floating clouds, without solid surface or the familiar boundaries between land and sky. Our instruments tell us that the swirling mass is almost totally hydrogen, and that, in the interior, because of the enormous atmospheric pressures, the gas takes on a totally new form: liquid metallic hydrogen. And now we can also see clearly the outermost moon of Jupiter, Callisto, displaying an enormous crater from which radiate concentric rings like frozen ripples in a gigantic pond. Next we come to Ganymede, Jupiter's largest moon, with its deeply grooved and mottled icy surface, and then Europa, strangely smooth except for some striations that may be fissures in its thick, icy crust. At this point we look for Almathea, an oddly shaped moon, and find it in a ring system that surrounds Jupiter, confirming the observation first made by our sister ship, *Voyager 1,* some months previously.

At this point, on day 647, we are directly adjacent Jupiter itself, and the famous Red Spot comes into view. It is like a giant geyser, an enormous column of complex gases forced up from the interior of the planet, a million-year-old Jovian storm. Next our attention is turned to another moon, called Io, brilliant with patches of red, orange, yellow, and black and pockmarked with the craters of many extinct volcanos. But wait, what is this? Yes, a volcano actually in the process of eruption, its bright plume outlined against the darker surface and a vast dust cloud, a hundred miles high, surrounding it. Here is another first: the first active volcano ever seen outside of our own Earth! And then on Day 662, feeling the boost from Jupiter's gravity, we reset course and are on our way to Saturn, some 780 days of travel away.

Thus far no planet or moon we have seen holds promise for sustaining life as we know it. Temperatures are too low, and the various atmospheres are devoid of oxygen. Thinking of all we have seen, we are filled with wonder at the magnitude of the great planet systems moving with clockwork precision around our sun, and staggered when we contemplate our solar system's place as a tiny pinpoint of matter in the vast universe. In this sense, too, the immensity and beauty of what we have seen suggests a new application of the words of Hebrews 12: "We are compassed about with so great a cloud of witnesses."[11]

On day 874 we have a brief scare as our guidance system malfunctions: we have lost our fix on the star Canopus! But ground control analyzes the trouble as a brief error of our optical sensors, which have mistaken Alpha and Beta Centauri for Canopus. Guidance is restored and we breathe more easily! At day 1350 we begin to see Saturn with its gigantic ring system looming up before us. Before the visit of our sister ship, *Voyager 1*, the intricacy of the ring system had not really been appreciated. We see the six major rings, and it seems that there is no real break in the continuity between them. Indeed, our photopolarimeter tells us that there are upward of 100,000 rings in the total system, far more than can be explained in terms of perturbations caused by the twenty or so of Saturn's satellites. As we come in close, at day 1429, we fire retro rockets to slow us down to 45,000 miles per hour, the speed of rotation of the outermost ring. We can now see some of the fine structure of the rings, and note that there is a dynamic variation in the density, as we look through the rings at the stars of Delta Scorpio. The density variation appears as some form of wave motion, and in the F ring, the innermost ring, the variations take on the appearance of a twisting or braiding of strands or ringlets. Finally, as we veer off from the whirling particles of dust and rock, snowballs and ice clumps, we see the spokes of the B ring, dark striations against the bright ring background. These curious lines extend about halfway through the ring in a radial fashion with respect to the planet.

Now we turn our attention to Saturn itself. It is reminiscent of Jupiter; though smaller, it is a vast assemblage of hydrogen and helium, with turbulent winds extending one thousand miles into its surface. Among its many satellites we see the prominent Titan, second largest satellite in our solar system. It is also the most interesting moon from our terrestrial perspective, because the chemistry of Titan may be similar to that of primitive Earth, a kind of early chapter of our own cosmic history. It looks mysterious, shrouded in clouds, with dark rings around its north pole. Its atmosphere, half the density of ours, is made up mostly of nitrogen and a smaller amount of methane. In its atmosphere are also traces of ethane, acetylene, ethylene, and hydrogen cyanide, presumably photochemical products of the sun's action on methane. Its surface temperature is $-289°F$. Perhaps we are looking at another place of the advent of life, but the low temperatures, resulting from the great distance from the sun, make that unlikely.

We have come to the end of our journey. At this point we must imagine disembarking from *Voyager 2,* just as it resets its course for a 1986 encounter with the planet Uranus. We have not gone this way before, so we can only guess at the wonders in the outer reaches of our solar system. But we have gone far enough to know that life as we know it is nowhere to be found. We are, for our sun, its only inhabited planet. Indeed, worlds are precious!

As for the rest of the cosmos, we can only wonder how many other worlds there are. Sagan has given estimates as high as 100 million, but narrows this drastically when considering technologically sophisticated cultures which, based upon our model, sadly jeopardize their own existence to perhaps only a few decades.

Walter Hearn, in his "Scientist's Psalm," takes a more joyous and optimistic view:

> Earth we live on, merely one
> Planet of a minor sun:
> Join this entire galaxy,
> Showing forth His majesty!
>
> Beyond our own galactic rim,
> Billions more are praising Him.
> Ten to some gigantic power
> Times the height of Babel's tower.
>
> Past the range of telescope:
> God of Faith and Love and Hope.
> Praise Him every tongue and race!
> Even those in outer space!
>
> Selah[12]

Gingerich takes an opposite but still reverent viewpoint, noting the narrow window for the advent of life on our planet and suggesting that we are alone in the cosmos, a unique production of the Designer.

Other scientists, taking a more anthropomorphic viewpoint, have explored the possibility that something intrinsic in the presence of intelligent life—in observer participation—actually serves as a moving force in the cosmos. In a 1973 conference at Cracow, Brandon Carter extrapolated from the anthropic principle to suggest that not only do the conditions prerequisite to human existence sharply constrain the range of possible observable universes, but the fundamental properties of force, space, and time are actually constrained to incorporate the evolution of intelligent observers.[13] John Wheeler, of the University of Texas, in the 1979 Einstein Centennial at Princeton, spoke of this universe-observer interaction as analogous to the way the delayed-choice experiment is carried out in quantum mechanics.[14] According to Henry Simmons, delayed-choice experiments in quantum physics involve an arbitrary decision on the part of the observer, while the experiment is still in progress, to observe the properties of electrons, photons, or other quantum entities in either a wavelike or particle-like manner.[15] John Wheeler describes the universe, based on this analogy, as a kind of self-excited circuit:

> Beginning with the Big Bang, the universe expands and cools. After eons of dynamic development, it gives rise to observership. Acts of observer-participance—via the mechanism of the delayed-choice experiment—in turn give tangible reality to the universe not only now but back to the beginning. To speak of the universe as a self-excited circuit is to imply once more a participatory universe.[16]

Other possible universes, if they lacked participatory observers, would, in Wheeler's view, be "stillborn." B. J. Carr and M. J. Rees, in a 1979 review article in *Nature,* elaborate on Wheeler's work as follows:

> Wheeler envisages an infinite ensemble of universes, all with different coupling constants and so on. Most are "stillborn," in the sense that the prevailing physical laws do not allow anything interesting to happen in them; only those which start off with the right constants can ever become "aware of themselves."[17]

Also present at the 1979 Einstein Centennial was physicist Freeman Dyson of the Institute for Advanced Study at Princeton. His summary of the ideas of the anthropic principle is lucid and searching:

> The idea of observer-participance is for Wheeler central to the understanding of nature. Observer-participance means that the universe must have built into it from the beginning the potentiality for containing observers. Without observers, there is no existence. The activity of observers in the remote future is foreshadowed in the remote past and guides the development of the universe throughout its history. The laws of physics evolve from initial chaos into the rigid structure of quantum mechanics because observers require a rigid structure for their operations. All this sounds to a contemporary physicist vague and mystical. But we should have learned by now that ideas that appear at first sight to be vague and mystical sometimes turn out to be true.

Wheeler is building on the work of Bob Dicke and Brandon Carter, who were the first to point out that the laws of physics and cosmology are constrained by the requirement that the universe should provide a home for theoretical physicists. Brandon Carter has shown that the existence of a long-lived star such as the sun, giving steady warmth to allow the slow evolution of life and intelligence, is only possible if the numerical constants of physics have values lying in a restricted range. Carter calls the requirement that the universe be capable of breeding physicists the "anthropic principle." Dicke and Carter have used the anthropic principle to set quantitative limits to the structure of the universe. Wheeler carries their idea much further, conjecturing that the laws of nature are not only quantitatively constrained but qualitatively molded by the existence of observers.

Wheeler united two streams of thought that had before been separate. On the one hand, in the domain of astronomy and cosmology, the anthropic principle of Dicke and Carter constrains the structure of the universe. On the other hand, in the domain of atomic physics, the laws of quantum mechanics take explicitly into account the fact that atomic systems cannot be described independently of the experimental apparatus by which they are observed in atomic physics; the reaction of the process of observation upon the object observed is an essential part of the description of the object.[18]

You may wonder, at this juncture of the material universe and the observer function of intelligent beings, just where all our exploration will lead. Are we product or cause; or is all this explained by a Higher Intelligence who has designed it all? We choose to think the latter, but hasten to add that he has much more for us to know. We can joyously join with Pascal when he says, "By space the universe encompasses and swallows me up like a dot; by thought I encompass the universe."[19]

UNDERSTANDING OUR ORIGINS

As our knowledge of the cosmos has grown, we have been increasingly confronted with staggering levels of order and immensity, a surprising correspondence between scientific and theological views, and exquisite preparation for the advent of intelligent life, all of which can only be attributable to a Designer. In a sense we have entered into the thought of the Designer, perhaps as a part of our legacy as the creation, as part of our *imago Dei*.

The process of human evolution, especially at the level of the contemplation of who we are and how we came to be here, has been called by philosophers the question of our century. There are those, like Jacques Monod, who see no special significance in the evolution of man, for, he says, we came as did the rest of the biosphere, "solely by chance."[20] But Arthur Peacocke impugns this as "false modesty, verging on intellectual perversity," suggesting, along with Polanyi, Eccles, and others, that the understanding of our own evolution is the most important issue confronting evolutionary theory.[21]

This process of understanding our evolution has recently become a concern of biological scientists interested in the thought process itself, at the level of the intricate details of the function of the human brain. Here again one is impressed with the enormous complexity and intricate interaction of the cells that make up the nervous system. Recall from Chapter 3 that anatomist Gareth Jones told us that the cerebral cortex contains 10^{10} to 10^{14} nerve cells, at least ten times Earth's human population, and that each nerve cell contacts more than five thousand other nerve cells through what are called synaptic junctions, with the information being transferred undergoing modification at each junction.[22]

As an example of this awesome "universe within," Gunther Stent describes for us the workings of the visual cortex in its interaction with the human eye as follows:

Information about the world reaches the brain, not as raw data but as highly processed structures that are generated by a set of stepwise, preconscious informational transformations of the sensory input . . . which "proceed according to a program that preexists in the brain." Transformation [of the light rays entering the eye] begins in the retina in the back of the eye. There a two-dimensional array of about a hundred million primary light receptor cells—the rods and the cones—converts the radiant energy of the image projected via the lens on the retina into a pattern of electrical signals, much as a television camera does. Since the electrical response of each light receptor cell depends on the intensity of light that happens to fall on it, the overall activity pattern of the light receptor cell array represents the light intensity existing at a hundred million different points in the visual space. The retina not only contains the input part of the visual sense, however, but also performs the first stage of the abstraction process. This first stage is carried out by another two-dimensional array of nerve cells, namely the million or so ganglion cells. The ganglion cells receive the electrical signals generated by the hundred million light receptor cells and subject them to information processing. The result of this processing is that the activity pattern of the ganglion cells constitutes a more abstract representation of the visual space than the activity pattern of the light receptor cells. Instead of reporting the light intensity existing at a single point in the visual space, each ganglion cell signals the light-dark contrast which exists between the center and the edge of a circular receptive field in the visual space, with each receptive field consisting of about a hundred contiguous points monitored by individual light receptor cells. In this way, the point-by-point fine-grained light intensity information is boiled down to a somewhat coarser field-by-field light contrast representation. As can be readily appreciated, such light contrast information is essential for the recognition of shapes and forms in space, or visual perception.

For the next stage of processing the visual information leaves the retina via the nerve fibers of the ganglion cells. These fibers connect the eye with the brain, and after passing a way station in the forebrain the output signals of the ganglion cells reach the cerebral cortex at the lower back of the head. Here the signals converge on a set of cortical nerve cells. Study of the cortical nerve cells receiving the partially abstracted visual input has shown that each of them responds only to light rays reaching the eye from a limited set of contiguous points in the visual space. But the structure of the receptive fields of these cortical nerve cells is more complicated and their size is larger than that of the receptive fields of the retinal ganglion cells. Instead of representing the light-dark contrast existing between the center and the edge of circular receptive fields, the cortical nerve cells signal the contrast which exists along straight line edges whose length amounts to many diameters of the circular ganglion cell receptive fields. A given cortical cell becomes active if a straight line edge of a particular orientation—horizontal, vertical, or oblique—formed by the border of contiguous areas of high and low light intensity is present in its receptive field. For instance, a vertical bar of light on a dark background in some part of the visual field may produce a vigorous response in a particular cortical nerve cell, and that response will cease if the bar is tilted away from the vertical or moved outside the receptive field. Thus the process of abstraction of the visual input begun in the retina is carried to higher levels in the cerebral cortex. At the first cortical abstraction stage the data supplied by the retinal ganglion cells concerning the light-dark contrast within small circular receptive fields are transformed into the more abstract data structure of contrast present along sets of circular fields arranged in straight lines.[23]

The exquisite connectedness that this relatively simple sensory process displays draws us back again to the question of design, of purpose and plan; of "pre-existing programs," as Stent calls it.

Indeed, it would seem that at every level in the cosmos, whether the astronomical ordering of light to stars to supernovae, or the microscopic cellular abstraction and transformation in the brain, or the delicate balance of the subatomic strong force holding atomic nuclei together, the hand of the Great Designer is far easier to see than to ignore. Perhaps it is supposed to be this way, at least for those who see and take off their shoes.

NOTES

1. Rom. 1:20. NIV.
2. Elizabeth Barrett Browning, "Aurora Leigh," *Complete Poetical Works of Elizabeth B. Browning, Book VII* (Boston: Houghton Mifflin, 1900).
3. Carl Sagan, *Cosmos* (New York: Random House, 1980), 5.
4. Owen Gingerich, Dwight lecture, University of Pennsylvania, April 6, 1982. Reprinted as "Let There Be Light: Modern Cosmogony and Biblical Creation" in *Is God a Creationist?*, ed. Roland M. Frye (New York: Scribners, 1983), 121.
5. Sagan, *Cosmos*, 4.
6. George Gale, "The Anthropic Principle," *Scientific American* 245 (1981): 2.
7. Henry Simmons, "Redefining the Universe," *Mosaic* 13 (March/April 1982): 18.
8. Ibid.
9. Gingerich, Dwight lecture, 1982.
10. Sagan, *Cosmos*, 5.
11. Heb. 12:1. KJV.
12. Walter Hearn, "Scientist's Psalm," *HIS Magazine*, 1963.
13. Brandon Carter, paper delivered at a conference commemorating the 500th anniv. of Copernicus's birth, at Cracow, 1973, referred to in Simmons, "Redefining the Universe," 16.

14. John Wheeler, paper delivered at Einstein Centennial, Princeton, 1979, referred to in Simmons, "Redefining the Universe," 19.
15. Simmons, "Redefining the Universe," 19.
16. In Simmons, "Redefining the Universe," 19.
17. Bernard J. Carr and Martin J. Rees, "The Anthropic Principle and the Structure of the Physical World," *Nature* 278 (12 April 1979): 605–12.
18. Freeman Dyson, paper delivered at Einstein Centennial, Princeton, 1979, referred to in Simmons, "Redefining the Universe," 20.
19. Blaise Pascal, *Pensees Great Books of the Western World,* vol 33, Encyclopedia Brittanica, (Chicago, 1952), 234.
20. Jacques Monod, *Chance and Necessity* (New York: Vintage Books, 1972), 59.
21. Arthur Peacocke, "Chance, Potentiality and God," in *Beyond Chance and Necessity,* ed. C. J. Lewis (Atlantic Highlands, N.J.: Humanities Press, 1974), 20.
22. Gareth Jones, *Our Fragile Brains* (Downers Grove, IL: InterVarsity Press, 1980), 38–39.
23. Gunther Stent, "The Promise of Structuralist Ethics," in vol. 6 of *The Hastings Center Report* (1976), 37–38.

5. The Vast Unseen and the Genetic Revolution

ON SEEING THE UNSEEN

God has woven a marvelous tapestry for the eyes of his creatures to behold. But in a sense we have lost a certain level of perception, a dimension of seeing, a sense of a Presence in the providential design of all that is. Michael Shallis of Oxford University notes this in a recent paper entitled "The Point of Cosmology," where he speaks of

> the change in perception occurring in the late Middle Ages. The allegorical world view was turning from a representation of man's relationship with the Creator and the cosmos to being a veil, masking reality. The real nature of things was seeming to become more material and less symbolic. Man's vision was being diverted from where the material signposts were pointing to an increasing desire to understand the "real" nature of the signposts.[1]

Yet the curious result for many who chose this focus for the search was the conclusion that there was nothing there! Nobel laureate physicist Steven Weinberg, for example, says that "the more the Universe seems comprehensible, the more it also seems pointless."[2] What does it take to see the hand of the Creator writing large in everything, regardless of its comprehensibility? Does it demand the eyes of faith, or is it there for anyone to see who will just allow the opportunity for reflection? C. S. Lewis argues in *The Abolition of Man* that our narrow approach to scientific truth threatens the existence of humankind. He calls for a "regenerate science," with the following character:

When it explained it would not explain away. When it spoke of the parts it would remember the whole. . . . Its followers would not be free with the words *only* and *merely*. In a word, it would conquer nature without being at the same time conquered by her and buy knowledge at a lower cost than that of life.[3]

The implication of these remarks is that the scientist is faced with a choice. The scientist may maintain a narrow, reductionist view of science, with the risk of depersonalization, or else may broaden his or her view to allow for an occasional enriching glimpse of the artistic, the poetic, the religious, as he or she surveys the implications of data.

The difficulty of the choice is presented by Alan Lightman in a *Science 82* article entitled "To The Dizzy Edge":

Most scientists will tell you there is a clear line between science and philosophy, between those questions that are answerable by logic and experiment and those that must forever float in the nethers of epistemology. Such is the heritage of Bacon and Galileo. Following this comfortable approach, *many of our finest biologists, chemists, and physicists have nestled into numbers for the duration.* And it's not surprising. In this strange and deep universe, humankind has an urgent *desire to know some few things with certainty.* But the philosophers will not leave us our scattered harbors. Listen to the persuasive words of Bertrand Russell, philosopher and master logician: "The observer, when he seems to himself to be observing a stone, is really, if physics is to be believed, observing the effects of the stone upon himself." What can we know, if not the world as it appears? And adding to our anxieties, modern science, through no fault of its own, repeatedly brings itself all the way to the dizzy edge of philosophy.

In the last few decades, science has plunged headlong after many other long-standing philosophical problems. An old debate is the question of free will versus determinism in human actions. The Heisenberg uncertainty principle in physics, stating that the trajectories of individual particles cannot be predicted precisely, has provided welcome ammunition to the free willists, while the studies of genes, DNA, and the newborn field of sociobiology surely put glee in the hearts of the determinists. And then there's the ancient controversy about whether mind is distinct from matter. I imagine the "mind-body problem" has had to take stock of recent developments in neurobiology, especially the results indicating that specific mental activities like language and emotions may be localized to specific halves of the brain. Science has not really answered any of these questions but continues to sharpen the focus.

And, no matter how far it progresses, science generates more questions than it answers. Questions that disturb. Perhaps there is in science an inevitable incompleteness, analogous to that in mathematics proved by Kurt Godel. Before Godel's proof, it was widely believed that each branch of mathematics, given sufficient axioms or rules of the game, was self-contained. In 1931 Godel rigorously demonstrated that arithmetic contains true theorems that cannot be derived from the rules of arithmetic. In a similar manner I believe there may be meaningful questions about physical reality, the territory of science, whose study is intrinsically beyond the reach of any equations or experiments.

In all these mysteries we see ourselves. Would we be so intrigued if we did not ponder why as well as how, if we did not have our Dalis and Sartres as well as our Madame Curies? This is surely a miracle, like the fragile balance of nuclear forces and the just-right release of the cosmic pendulum.[4]

And so we plead with those who have "nestled into numbers for the duration" to look beyond the numbers to see the object, the process, the model, the phenomenon as part of a larger, more marvelous, and mysterious whole. Albert Einstein, perhaps the greatest scientist who ever lived, was forever fond of contrasting his mathematics with his aesthetic view of reality. Timothy Ferris quotes him in an October *Science 83* article:

"I want to know how God created this world. I want to know his thoughts, the rest are details."

Ferris goes on to say,

Einstein saw God as dressed in questions more than answers—"What really interests me," he told his assistant Ernst Straus, "is whether God had any choice in the creation of the world"—and his personality was imbued with a deep sense of the mysterious. "The most beautiful experience we can have is the mysterious," he said. "It is the fundamental emotion that stands at the cradle of true art and true science. Whoever does not know it is as good as dead, and his eyes are dimmed."[5]

Similarly, K. C. Cole writes in an article entitled "The Scientific Aesthetic":

Artists approach nature with feeling; scientists rely on logic. Art elicits emotion; science makes sense. Artists are supposed to care; scientists are supposed to think.

At least one physicist I know rejects this distinction out of hand: "What a strange misconception has been taught to people," he says. "They have been taught that one cannot be disciplined enough to discover the truth unless one is indifferent to it. Actually, there is no point in looking for the truth unless what it is makes a difference."

The history of science bears him out. Darwin, while sorting out the clues he had gathered in the Galapagos Islands that eventually led to his theory of evolution, was hardly detached. "I am like a gambler and love a wild experiment," he wrote. "I am horribly afraid. I trust to a sort of instinct and God knows can seldom give any reason for my remarks. All nature is perverse and will not do as I wish it. I wish I had my old barnacles to work at, and nothing new." The scientists who took various sides in the early days of the quantum debate were scarcely less passionate. Einstein said that if classical notions of cause and effect had to be renounced, he would rather be a cobbler or even work in a gambling casino than be a physicist. Niels Bohr called Einstein's attitude appalling, and accused him of high treason. Another major physicist, Erwin Schroedinger, said, "If one has to stick to this damned quantum jumping, then I regret having ever been involved in this thing." On a more positive note, Einstein spoke about the universe as a "great, eternal riddle" that "beckoned like a liberation." As the late Harvard professor George Sarton wrote in the preface to his *History of Science,* "There are blood and tears in geometry as well as in art."[6]

Cole's physicist friend is surely on the right track. *What truth is makes a difference!* There neither is nor should be a prohibition on the subjective, the poetic, or the religious in the scientist's quest for truth. Perhaps Nobel laureate Richard Feynman says it best in a poem quoted by K. C. Cole:

Poets say science takes away from the beauty of the stars—mere globs of gas atoms. Nothing is "mere." I too can see the stars on a desert night, and feel them. But do I see less or more? The vastness of the heavens stretches my imagination—stuck on this carrousel, my little eye can catch one-million-year-old light. . . . For far more marvelous is the truth than any artists of the past imagined! Why do the poets of the present not speak of it? What men are poets who can speak of Jupiter if he were like a man, but if he is an immense spinning sphere of methane and ammonia must be silent?[7]

And what of religion? How have we come to the point where science and theology seem so utterly divorced from each other? One of us spoke to this question in a Yale Medical School address some years ago.

Paul Tillich once referred to this age (our culture) as "the land of broken symbols." That break is at least partly science derived, based upon the assumption that objective scientific study would produce a complete description of all of reality and preclude any other source of truth as outmoded and irrelevant. So, the little boy would say, "Science is material and religion is immaterial." And so, scientists and theologians have gone their separate ways.

It was a sad parting, I feel, because each discipline had done so much for the other. It is no mistake that science came out of a Christian culture, for example. For the biblical perspective of an utterly trustworthy Creator whose universe was ordered and rational was essential to the scientists' expectation of meaningful experimentation. As Einstein later wrote, "God who creates and is nature, is very difficult to understand but He is not arbitrary or malicious." Then, too, to be a scientist was an honorable and worthy occupation, in contrast to the pagan idea of science: Prometheus stealing fire from the gods, who were jealous of mortal man's possession of their knowledge. Biblically, man is presented as a creature of God and his work, as part of the Divine unfolding, to have dominion over the earth, always with the proviso to love God and neighbor. So the scientist is no unwelcome interloper but a servant-son in his Father's creation. As Oxford's Charles Coulson once said, the practice of science is to be seen as a fit activity for a Sabbath afternoon.

Science, in return, has given the theologian a real world. As Walter Thorson has expressed it, "medieval society and medieval thought were . . . centered on a fundamentally religious conceptual framework with a papier-mâché sort of physical universe which had no more meaning than a kind of 'stage prop' on which the drama of salvation was enacted." By comparison, science "took the secular world and the secular calling more seriously. Instead of a *papier-mâché* universe, God had made a real one, and the basic inspiration for the scientific revolution was a passionate belief that, in exploring and knowing what God had given us men in creation, we would find a larger framework in which our grasp of our role and destiny—could grow and develop further."

The challenge came in the words of Francis Bacon, "if . . . there be any humility towards the Creator, if there be any reverence for or disposition to magnify His works, if there be any charity for man . . . we should approach with humility and veneration to unroll the volume of Creation." Science thus came as an outgrowth of religious concern, not as a competitor but rather as a complementary activity, to enlarge our view of God's Creation.[8]

And what of the study of genes, DNA, and sociobiology? Do they, as Lightman suggests, really support an impersonal deterministic philosophy? We think not. For here again, it would seem, God is weaving a tapestry of richness, beauty, and intricacy. And it seems an ever-growing, dynamic phenomenon, this structure of truth, this "volume of Creation."

THE GENETIC REVOLUTION

The explosive increase in our knowledge of the gene began in a quiet little garden in an Austrian monastery in the city of Brunn in 1865. The experimenter was Gregor Mendel, a monk, and his ten years of work, presented at the Natural History Society of Brunn, was scarcely noticed. But what Mendel had discovered was earthshaking: characteristics in his pea plants, such as seed color or shape, and pod color or shape, were inherited as separate entities and were expressed in either of two ways—dominant or recessive.

Dominance was observed in the first genetic cross. If, for example, plants with smooth seeds were crossed with plants having wrinkled seeds, then the first, or F_1, generation displayed only one of the two seed shapes, that of the smooth, or dominant, character. Crossing hybrid plants led to a surprising result: the reappearance of the "missing" or recessive characteristic—unchanged—in one-quarter of the progeny. Mendel's conclusion, that there existed a fundamental unit of heredity, was expressed in his now-famous paper as follows:

The constant characters that appear in the group of plants may be obtained in all the associations that are possible according to the mathematical laws of combination. Those characters which are transmitted visibly, and therefore constitute the characters of the hybrid, are termed the dominant, and those that become latent in the process are termed recessive. The expression "recessive" has been chosen because such characters withdraw or disappear entirely in the hybrids, but nevertheless reappear unchanged in their progeny in predictable proportions, without any essential alterations. Transitional forms were not observed in any experiment.[9]

But Mendel's discoveries were not appreciated until 1903, when a visual basis for inheritance came about with the discovery of chromosomes as structures with properties that corresponded with Mendel's units of inheritance. Chromosomes were observed prior to cell division to be divided longitudinally into two copies, and each copy to be subsequently pulled toward opposite poles of the cell. In this way each daughter cell received one copy of each chromosome—a complete set of genetic instructions.

The nonprotein components of genetic material had been the subject of a study, carried out by Friedrich Miescher in Basel, around the time Mendel was doing his work. Miescher had studied the nuclear material from two very different sources: the sperm of the Rhine salmon and pus cells from bandages from the local hospital. Both contained a substance he called nuclein, which many years later was shown to be DNA. He also described another component of the salmon sperm, a basic protein called protamine. Protamine had the usual structure of a protein molecule, a long series of amino acids linked to each other in so-called peptide linkage, but there was a preponderance of basic amino acids—arginine, lysine, and histidine.

These, then, were understood as the fundamental components of the chromosome: a variety of basic proteins called protamines and histones and some less-well-characterized organic phosphorus compounds.

The genetic aspect was generally assumed to reside in the protein components, but in 1944 O. T. Avery and his collaborators at what was then the Rockefeller Institute, now Rockefeller University, demonstrated that a strain of the pneumonia-causing bacterium, pneumococcus, could be transformed from a nonvirulent to a virulent type by means of a nonprotein component of chromosomelike material obtained from the virulent type. This substance was the highly polymerized phosphorus-containing compound deoxyribonucleic acid (DNA). Avery's description of the isolation of this curious substance, which had somehow never been suspected of being present in pneumococcus, reads as follows:

When alcohol reaches a concentration of about 9/10 volume there separates out a fibrous substance which on stirring the mixture wraps itself about the glass rod like thread on a spool and the other impurities stay behind as a granular precipitate. The fibrous material is redissolved and the process repeated several times. In short, this substance is highly reactive and on elementary analysis conforms very closely to the theoretical values of pure DNA (who could have guessed it). This type of nucleic acid has not to my knowledge been recognized in *Pneumococcus* before, although it has been found in other bacteria.[10]

Avery's conclusion on the induction of virulence, which is accompanied by the appearance of a new cell surface polysaccharide, is also interesting.

The inducing substance, on the basis of its chemical and physical properties, appears to be a highly polymerized and viscous form of DNA. On the other hand, the type III capsular substance, the synthesis of which is evoked by this transforming agent, consists chiefly of a nonnitrogenous polysaccharide. . . . Thus it is evident that the inducing substance and the substance produced in turn are chemically distinct and biologically specific in their action and that both are requisite in determining the type specificity of the cells of which they form a part.[11]

The unique character of DNA as the conveyer of hereditary information was finally and unequivocally established in 1953 with the publication of the Watson-Crick model for DNA. The structure of DNA suggested its hereditary role: two helical chains in which nitrogenous bases attached to the sugar-phosphate backbone of each chain were bonded to each other by weak so-called hydrogen bonds. The bases were of four kinds, called adenine (A), guanine (G), cytosine (C), and thymine (T), and bonding was specific. Each time an A appeared in one chain, a T was found opposite it. Likewise, each time a G occurred in one chain, a C was on the other. This system of complementary base-pair formation—A always opposite T and G opposite C—suggested the basis of a hereditary mechanism. If the chains of nucleotides—as bases attached to their sugar-phosphates were called—were separated, and a new copy of each fashioned according to the base-pairing rules, the original molecule would be exactly reproduced. Presumably, too, the sequence of bases in the polymer was the information content of the molecule. Studies of mutation in which a single base was changed showed that the exact linear sequence was essential for proper functioning of the gene.

The story of how Watson and Crick arrived at the structure of DNA reads more like a spy thriller than a scientific book.[12] In one of the great ironies of scientific research, the principal contributors of the data—Rosalind Franklin, the crystallographer whose data revealed the double helix, and Erwin Chargaff, the organic chemist who discovered the equality of A and T and of G and C—were bypassed, essentially by their own choice. They simply did not take the biochemist James Watson and his physicist friend Francis Crick—a kind of scientific odd couple—seriously. Indeed, Chargaff has become an outspoken critic of the entire genetic enterprise, pointing to the way in which its practitioners have sought to explain away the mysteries of nature. He writes in his autobiography, *Heraclitean Fire,*

If it is the real purpose of science to teach us true things about nature, to reveal to us the reality of the world, the consequences of such teaching ought to be increased wisdom, a greater love of nature, and, in a few, a heightened admiration of divine power. By confronting us directly with something incommensurably greater than ourselves, science should serve to push back the confines of the misery of human existence. These are the effects it may have had on men like Kepler or Pascal. But science, owing to the operation of forces that nobody, I believe, can disentangle, has not persisted in this direction. From an undertaking designed to understand nature, it has changed into one attempting to explain, and then to improve on, nature.[13]

Chargaff's conclusion, although somewhat embittered (he says of himself that he was born with a stone in his shoe), is a sobering one. It would seem that molecular genetics fits the mold of that unregenerate science that C. S. Lewis has described. Wondrous discovery seems always tainted by a certain arrogance.

But once DNA's role in heredity had been established, another question loomed large. If DNA was the genetic material, then its role must be to direct the synthesis of all the cell's proteins. Yet protein synthesis was known to occur in the cell's cytoplasm, and DNA was restricted to the cell nucleus. How, then, did DNA transmit its instructions?

The answer to this question was first formulated by François Jacob and Jacques Monod, two French biochemists working at the Pasteur Institute. They were studying a fascinating bacterial phenomenon called induction, in which a new degradative enzyme was produced by growing cells when a substance was introduced into the culture medium that could be broken down and utilized for growth under the agency of that degradative enzyme. Furthermore, the process was reversible. On removal of the substance serving as a food source, the degradative enzyme quickly disappeared from the bacterial cells. Perhaps the most interesting aspect was that the induction process was under genetic control. The gene that produced the degradative enzyme was regulated by a second, closely linked gene. The French biochemists hypothesized that the gene producing the degradative enzyme was copied to form an intermediate template that was unstable, being constantly broken down and resynthesized. This molecule was proposed to be made up of ribonucleic acid (RNA), a close relative of DNA, which had been found in high concentration at the site of protein synthesis in growing bacteria.

Subsequently it was shown in several laboratories that DNA was actually copied into a polymer called messenger RNA (mRNA), again through complementary base-pairing to ensure a faithful copy, by an enzyme system called RNA polymerase. Enzymes called DNA polymerases had previously been described which were responsible for copying DNA; they used so-called deoxynucleoside triphosphates, activated forms of the A, T, G, and C bases attached to the sugar unique to DNA, 2-deoxyribose. The RNA polymerase used a similar set of precursor molecules, A, U (uracil), G, and C, but this time the sugar was ribose instead of deoxyribose. Verification that this mRNA molecule was the "transcript" of the genetic material was obtained by demonstrating its movement from the site of synthesis in the nucleus to the protein-synthetic machinery in the cytoplasm. This machinery consisted of a complex structure called a polysome, made up of a series of so-called ribosomes attached to the long mRNA molecule, like pearls on a necklace.

It had also been shown that there was a direct linear relationship between the DNA sequence of a given gene and the amino acid sequence of the protein for which that gene coded. How, then, was the mRNA sequence in the cytoplasm translated into the sequence of its protein product? There needed to be adapter molecules that could "read" the sequence of bases in the mRNA and then introduce the correct amino acid into the protein chain at each point. It was found that this function was performed by another type of RNA molecule, called transfer RNA (tRNA). This molecule was two-headed, as might be expected for an adapter; one end carried the specific amino acid and the other carried a series of bases that served as a recognition point for a particular three-base sequence in the mRNA. Each tRNA had its unique anticodon recognition site, unique to the amino acid it carried. So, for example, the mRNA sequence CCC dictated the binding of a tRNA with the anticodon GGG, which carried at its other end the amino acid proline. Every time CCC appeared in the mRNA sequence, a proline-tRNA would bind by base-pairing of its GGG anticodon to the mRNA codon CCC, and its proline would be introduced into the protein chain. In the total code word dictionary, there are sixty-one combinations of three bases that code for a specific amino acid, and three others that signal the termination of protein chains. Almost all the amino acids have more than one code word, hence more than one tRNA carrying that amino acid. This degeneracy, as it is called, presumably allows for some mutations to occur without leading to errors in the sequence of amino acids in the protein. The code has been shown to be universal. All species of organisms use the same code word dictionary.

Here, then, in outline, is the state of our knowledge of molecular genetics. The future of genetic research, its application in medicine, agriculture, and industry, for the benefit of humankind, is tremendously promising. Already our knowledge of the hereditary mechanism has opened up new avenues of investigation in understanding cellular differentiation, and the dedifferentiation that occurs when tissues become cancerous. New insights into the production of the antibodies that protect us from invasive agents and tumor-forming cells are forthcoming.

One of the most powerful tools of the trade is gene splicing, a process whereby genes from different sources can be joined in new combinations for study of their interaction or for amplification of a given gene sequence. The key step in the process is the application of a unique group of enzymes called restriction endonucleases, which cut the DNA double helix in a special way to yield what are called sticky ends. Two different DNA molecules so treated can then be mixed and joined in new combinations never before possible. One such new possibility, foundational for the whole process, is the subsequent joining of the DNA molecules of interest with a special DNA structure called a plasmid. Plasmids are circular DNA molecules found in certain bacterial strains as a separate replicating element, like a miniature chromosome. When opened by treatment with restriction enzymes, they too form sticky ends, and, after joining with the new DNA combination under study, can be reintroduced into the bacterium and allowed to reproduce. In this way the new DNA sequence introduced into the plasmid may be replicated thousands of times, thereby providing large amounts of that particular gene for study. Genetic engineering applications include the treatment of genetic disease, production of new plants for increased world food production, and design of new bacteria to break down industrial pollutants.

One of the most exciting opportunities provided by the new genetic techniques is the study of the numerous cellular proteins for which no known function exists. The enormous resolving power of the gene-splicing approach is brought to bear on these unknown substances by making use of the fundamental molecular relationship between the synthesis of DNA, RNA, and proteins that we have just reviewed. The process begins with the isolation of a new protein molecule in order to study its structure and cellular function. As in most cases, the amount of material available for study is minuscule, but there are, because of molecular genetics, some new tricks to play.

One approach is to determine a short part of the protein sequence of the new protein, perhaps a length of six amino acids at one end. This can be done with a few micrograms of the protein. Then a "gene" is synthesized in a DNA synthesizer with the proper sequence to code for the six amino acids: eighteen nucleotides in the sequence, each triplet the complementary sequence to the mRNA codon for that amino acid in the code word dictionary. This eighteen-unit DNA sequence, radioactively labeled to allow for its subsequent identification, is then introduced into an extract of the total cellular RNA of the species from which the unknown protein had been obtained. In this extract are all the mRNAs of the cell, and the eighteen-nucleotide-long DNA fragment selects from the entire mixture the only completely complementary sequence, that of the mRNA coding for the unknown protein, and forms a stable DNA-RNA hybrid of the kind that forms transiently during the process of transcription. Because this is the only DNA-RNA hybrid in the extract, nuclear DNA having been excluded, the unique binding characteristic of double-stranded nucleic acids allows for a separation of this molecule from the rest of the cellular RNA.

Actually the molecule as it emerges from the separation process is still mostly single-stranded mRNA, but with an eighteen-nucleotide section at one end bound to the synthesized DNA fragment. This structure can now be converted to a completely double-stranded hybrid DNA-RNA molecule by means of another enzyme, found in certain viruses, called reverse transcriptase. This enzyme, as its name indicates, can take an RNA template and make a DNA-RNA hybrid, given the appropriate activated building blocks, the deoxynucleoside triphosphates. In this way the entire mRNA molecule is converted to a hybrid structure; the mRNA has been reconverted to the form of one strand of *its original gene!* Now we can separate the two chains, and treat the DNA single strand with DNA polymerase to generate the double-stranded DNA, its form as a gene.

In the double-stranded form DNA can now be spliced into a bacterial plasmid, as outlined earlier, and the plasmid placed in a bacterium and multiplied. After large-scale growth of the bacterium, the plasmid can be reisolated, and the DNA, coding for the unknown protein, introduced into a protein-synthetic system for the large-scale synthesis of the still-unknown protein.

The tremendous resolving power of the molecular genetic system is now apparent. All that is needed in this case is a tiny fragment of information—a six-amino-acid sequence of a huge protein molecule—and we can synthesize the entire protein in large quantities for detailed studies of its structure and function.

This, then, is the present state of our understanding of the molecular biology of the gene. It is amusing to speculate on how Gregor Mendel might have reacted if he were suddenly thrust into our era and given a molecular biological explanation for his genetic experiments. When he observed the results of his pioneer experiments with smooth and wrinkled peas, he could never have dreamed of the drama that was acted out within the intricate structures of his garden plants. The pollen grains that he took with a fine camel's hair brush from the stamens of a smooth-pea plant, when dusted on the stigma of a wrinkled-pea plant, actually introduced into the plant's reproductive apparatus a molecule of DNA. This molecule, it turned out, was responsible for Mendel's observation of the invariable formation of hybrid plants, which produced only smooth-pea seeds.

The mechanism of this kind of inherited change constitutes one of the most fascinating processes ever elucidated in the natural sciences. As we follow the DNA molecule from its source in the pollen grain into the recipient plant's reproductive apparatus, the first step in the process is an interaction with the tissues of the stigma and the swelling and germination of the pollen grain. A pollen tube then forms and penetrates the ovary at the base of the stigma. The sperm cell, carrying its DNA molecule, enters the embryo sac and fertilization occurs. Complex mechanisms ensure that only one pollen tube enters the ovule, regardless of the number of pollen grains that germinate.

Fertilization brings the sperm cell into close association with an egg cell in the embryo sac. The DNA molecule of the sperm cell and the corresponding DNA molecule of the egg cell are then brought together, and the result is a new cell with two copies of each gene of the pea plant, one gene copy from each of the two DNA molecules. Included in this genetic repertoire are, of course, the gene sequence encoding the instructions for smooth-pea seed coats from the sperm and wrinkled-pea seed coats from the egg. How, then, do the results of this combination, the hybrid plants, finally yield only offspring with smooth-seed coats? Mendel had talked about dominant and recessive factors in the expression of seed coat shape, but what was happening at the molecular level? The gene sequence dictating smooth-pea seed coat carried information for the conversion of all seed coat components into the variety producing smooth peas. But to do this a vast panorama of events were first necessary. To begin with, the single fertilized egg had to undergo a series of cell divisions, each time first duplicating its two DNA molecules and then segregating them into the daughter cells in such a way that a perfect copy of each of the original DNA molecules appeared in each. The process of duplication of the DNA molecules, mediated by a DNA polymerase, is enormously complicated in higher organisms. The DNA of the pea plant, as in all higher organisms, is present in all its cells in the form of a complex DNA-protein structure called chromatin. The fundamental unit of the chromatin is a beadlike structure called a nucleosome, which is composed of several kinds of histone proteins surrounded by several coils of the double-helical DNA. In its extended form, as, for example, during replication, the chromatin looks like a string of beads, the individual nucleosomes linked to each other by connecting segments of the continuous DNA double helix. At other times the chromatin structure is more tightly folded into helical structures in which the subunit is made up of six tightly associated nucleosomes. In this form there are approximately one thousand lengths of DNA per unit length of chromatin.

Because the protein components provide stability and assistance in folding during formation of the chromosomal structures essential to cell division, it is equally essential that the integrity of chromatin be maintained during DNA duplication. The mechanical requirements of this process are staggering. To begin with, the DNA molecule in higher plants carries about two billion base pairs and has an overall length of about sixty cm. Given the fact that the average plant cell is microscopic in size, the DNA molecule must be highly folded and compact. Yet for copying to occur, this structure must be unfolded at least transiently, and also unwound, because the DNA is still in a double-helical form. The copying by DNA polymerase occurs at a rate of one thousand base pairs per minute, with as many as ten thousand polymerase molecules functioning at different points along the long DNA-protein structure. The complexity of this unfolding-untwisting process is awesome, given the highly compact state of chromatin, the simultaneous copying at ten thousand points, and the high rate of movement of the polymerase molecules. One turn of the double-helical structure is duplicated each second, and the process is complete in three and one-half hours. A midsummer carnival night is dull by comparison with this spectacle!

Then, in order for cell division to occur, the two newly formed duplex DNA molecules must be completely separated and then divided into the fourteen chromosomal segments characteristic of the pea plant at cell division. This part of the process, because of its visibility in the light microscope, is more familiar to us. Yet even here the molecular events, involving the enormous compacting of the chromatin and the formation and movement of the mitotic spindle, which aligns and then separates the pairs of chromosomes, are staggering in their complexity. The chromosomes of the pea plant are formed from chromatin by a supercoiling process in which the already tightly wound nucleosomal arrays are wrapped back and forth in a process that is like making a narrow compress out of a roll of bandage. At this level there are ten thousand lengths of DNA per unit length of chromosome! As for the other components involved in cell division, we are only now elucidating the structure of the contractile proteins of the spindle fibers, and we have only the barest understanding of the microfilaments in the cell cytoplasm, which they presumably work against to effect the movement of chromosomes and the formation of the new cell membranes of the daughter cells.

Thus far we have followed our DNA molecule through one stage of division of the fertilized egg, and this process must be repeated many times to produce the mature seed in the pea pod. But what of the read-out of the DNA molecules' genetic information? How is the information of the DNA molecule of the sperm cell finally utilized to bring about the morphological change in the seed? For this to happen, processes of transcription of the DNA into messenger RNA and then translation into protein must occur. The latter process has been well characterized over the past decade, but the process of transcription is only now beginning to be described for higher organisms. It begins in the cell nucleus with the synthesis of an RNA transcript of the DNA. This molecule is a precursor of mRNA, and contains, in addition to the sequence of codons that will be used for protein assembly, a series of internal sequences that must be removed before the molecule leaves the nucleus. At present we have no hint as to the function of these internal sequences, or "introns," but they are present in most genes of the DNA of higher organisms. Our gene for the synthesis of the smooth-seed coat will therefore first need to have its intron sequences removed and the coding sections spliced together in precise order for the sequence of protein to be produced. The picture is one of a long RNA molecule being generated from the DNA template—with transient unwinding and separation of component nucleosomes in the chromatin matrix, as with replication—and the sequential excision of intron sequences and resplicing of adjacent coding sequences as the RNA bends and folds to bring each succeeding intron into the proper form for action. It is analogous to a giant steel fabrication plant in which massive wheels and conveyer belts cooperate to twist and turn, unwind and rewind, bend and stretch, open and close mile-long sections of a fifty-mile-long flexible steel bar to produce a half-mile-long finished product!

But our pea-seed coat mRNA is not ready yet! After transcription, a special enzyme introduces a long sequence of adenine nucleotides to form a polyA tail. We are not certain what the function of this structure is, though mRNA molecules with the polyA are more stable. At the same time, a second enzyme system works on the head-end of the mRNA molecule to add a short sequence called a cap. The cap generally involves a G nucleotide and sometimes added methyl groups. In our pea-seed coat mRNA molecule there would be a methyl group on the G nucleotide and another on the next base in the sequence.

At this point the completed mRNA is transported to the site of protein synthesis in the cytoplasm. Special proteins then combine with the mRNA, perhaps to enhance ribosome binding. Ribosomes then attach at appropriate points, and tRNAs with their attached amino acids come into play as dictated by the mRNA sequence. The growing protein chain, as it elongates and extends from the polyribosomal structure, is channeled through the cell membrane surface so that modification of the seed coat components can occur on location.

And so ends the journey of our gene for a smooth-pea seed coat; reproduced and transcribed, and then the transcript modified and translated, and then the protein product delivered to the seed. The total number of steps in all these processes exceeds many hundreds, and almost all have their origin in a specific gene as well. We have touched on only a few of the most important steps. We have not touched on the myriad of events involved in the process of embryogenesis, whereby that single fertilized egg differentiates into all the tissues of the plant. But at present there is little known of this process from a molecular standpoint.

SCIENCE IN HISTORICAL PERSPECTIVE

If and when we have completed our exploration of this vast complexity, will we be tempted to say that we have explained it? Does our mechanistic explanation really suffice? Certainly it did not suffice in the minds of many of the early scientists, who found in their work the opportunity to explore God's creation, and a larger framework in which to grasp their role and destiny. Malcolm Dixon, world-renowned biochemist of King's College, Cambridge, spoke of the religious faith of some of these pioneers in an address at a meeting of the British Association.

Robert Boyle, who . . . might as much as any man be called the founder of chemistry . . . also played an important part in the foundation of the Royal Society. He stated that he found few atheists among men of science. He wrote much on the relations between Christianity and science and learned Hebrew and Greek in order to study the Scriptures. He gave away a large part of his income for Church and missionary work, spent large sums on translations of the Bible, and by his will founded the Boyle lectures for the defence of Christianity against attacks.

. . . Kepler, the great astronomer, . . . worked out the laws of motion of the planets which were employed by Sir Isaac Newton in his great work on gravitation. He believed that in discovering natural laws he was, as he put it, "thinking God's thoughts after Him."

Newton himself was perhaps not quite orthodox, but he was a firm believer in God and in the Bible, and wrote a great deal on theology and on biblical interpretation. I need not remind you of the tremendous importance of his contributions to science: gravitation, the laws of motion, astronomy (especially of the solar system), the tides, optics, the telescope, spectroscopy, the nature of light, the differential calculus—these are only some of the subjects on which his work makes him the greatest British scientist of all time. One of his letters throws some light on the motives behind his work. Writing about his great work, the *Principia,* he says, "When I wrote my Treatise about our system, I had an Eye upon such principles as might work with considering men for the Belief of a Deity and nothing can rejoice me more than to find it useful for that Purpose."[14]

Dixon then goes on to extend the list of eminent physicists: Michael Faraday, Lord Kelvin, Sir George Stokes, Clerk Maxwell, Lord Rayleigh, and J. J. Thomson, each of whom was a devout believer.

As to the faith of other groups of scientists, he goes on to say,

At Cambridge in the first half of the 19th century there was little or no science; the credit for creating an interest in science there is due to two deeply religious men, Adam Sedgwick, Professor of Geology, and J. S. Henslow, Professor of Botany. Professor Coulson mentioned last year how Sedgwick preached to the miners at Newcastle. It was Henslow who got Darwin interested in science, and Darwin spoke of his deep religious sense. It seems that Darwin himself was a believer at the time when he did his great work on the origin of species. In that book he speaks of the laws impressed on matter by the Creator and of life having been originally breathed into a few forms or into one, and he prefixed to the book a quotation from Bacon, "Let no man think . . . that a man can . . . be too well studied in the book of God's work, or in the book of God's works." Later, however, he tells us rather sadly that he gave up his faith and subsequently even lost all appreciation of beauty in poetry, music and art. Alfred Russel Wallace, who independently arrived at the same conclusions as Darwin, and at the same time, was certainly an orthodox believer.

The list of religious people in the fields of biology and medicine also includes Lord Lister, Sir James Simpson, Edward Jenner, Louis Pasteur, and Gregor Mendel. Dixon concludes:

LINCOLN CHRISTIAN COLLEGE AND SEMINARY 80433

These men largely *made* the scientific method and yet were firm believers in Christianity, and they were not aware of any inconsistency.

The stock explanation advanced by those who believe that religion and science are irreconcilable is that they must have kept their religion and their science in watertight compartments in their minds. But there is not the slightest evidence for this, and as we have seen in many cases there is evidence that this was not so. It would be much truer to say that they approached their research in the spirit of the "research worker's text," that text which Lord Rayleigh prefixed to his collected scientific papers and which is carved on the great door of the Cavendish Laboratory, "The works of the Lord are great, sought out of all them that have pleasure therein."[15]

Perhaps we will be tempted to say that our scientific forebears knew much less than we. Clearly our knowledge of the gene has grown a thousandfold beyond what Mendel could have even dreamed! Yet in all their magnificent complexity, present scientific descriptions seem to be only partial and tentative pictures of what we are studying. There is, in fact, a strong feeling that there may be another whole layer or level of detail behind every process we have examined, so that the aggregate may be another thousand-fold level of complexity yet to be explored!

As Lincoln Barnett says in *The Universe and Dr. Einstein,*

In the evolution of scientific thought, one fact has become impressively clear: there is no mystery of the physical world which does not point to a mystery beyond itself. . . . Man's inescapable impasse is that he himself is part of the world he seeks to explore; his body and proud brain are mosaics of the same elemental particles that compose the dark drifting clouds of interstellar space; he is, in the final analysis, merely an ephemeral conformation of the premordial space-time field. Standing midway between macrocosm and microcosm, he finds barriers on every side and can perhaps but marvel, as St. Paul did nineteen hundred years ago, that the world was created by the word of God so that what is seen was made out of things which do not appear.[16]

What, then, of the Author of this magnificent work? How do we view our Creator in light of all the ever-multiplying complex-

80433

ity and diversity that confronts us? Can we not see him as grander and mightier than we ever dreamed?

As St. Paul also reminds us, "For since the creation of the world God's invisible qualities—his eternal power and divine nature—have been clearly seen, being understood from what has been made."[17]

NOTES

1. Michael Shallis, "The Point of Cosmology," *Irish Astronomical Journal* 15 (1982): 266.
2. Steven Weinberg, *The First Three Minutes* (London: Fontane, 1977), 149.
3. C. S. Lewis, *The Abolition of Man* (Oxford: Oxford University Press, 1943), 47.
4. Alan Lightman, "To The Dizzy Edge," *Science 82* (October 1982): 25–26.
5. Timothy Ferris, "The Other Einstein," *Science 83* (October 1983): 39.
6. K. C. Cole, "The Scientific Aesthetic," *Discover* (December 1983): 62–63.
7. Ibid., 62.
8. Robert L. Herrmann, "On Taking Vows in Two Priesthoods, Christianity and Science," *Yale Journal of Biology and Medicine* 49 (1976): 455–59.
9. Gregor Mendel, "The Birth of Genetics," papers in English translation, *Genetics* 35 (1950): Supp., 1–47.
10. O. T. Avery, C. M. MacLeod, and J. McCarty, "Studies on the Chemical Nature of the Substance Inducing Transformation in Pneumococcal Types," *Journal of Experimental Medicine* 79 (1944): 137–58.
11. Ibid.
12. James D. Watson, *The Double Helix* (New York: Atheneum, 1968).
13. Erwin Chargaff, *Heraclitean Fire* (New York: Rockefeller University Press, 1978), 120.
14. Malcolm Dixon, *Science and Irreligion* (London: Falcon Booklets, 1953), 5–6.
15. Ibid., 6–7.
16. Lincoln Barnett, *The Universe and Dr. Einstein* (New York: Signet, 1957), 115-16.
17. Rom. 1:20, NIV.

6. Deep and Powerful Ordering Forces in the Universe

THE ORDERING PRINCIPLE

Ancient ideas of divine order in the universe were mostly polytheistic notions of a nature influenced in an arbitrary way by competing deities. By contrast, the Old Testament description of Genesis presents a picture of a single, all-powerful deity, whose creative activity is orderly, purposeful, and good. The New Testament lends even greater distinction to the work of this transcendent God by revealing his ongoing concern for the order of this material world he has made. The Apostle Paul, in his letter to the Colossians, and the writer of the letter to the Hebrews both emphasize the immanent activity of God in his universe ("By Him all things consist"; "He upholds all things by the word of His power."[1]

The significance of this ordering principle has been increasingly appreciated with the development of relativity theory, through the major philosophical upheaval of quantum theory and the uncertainty principle, and in the current studies of the relationship of order to disorder by Mitchell Feigenbaum, Ilya Prigogine, and David Bohm. It is becoming increasingly evident that there are deep and powerful forces stipulating order in the universe.

HISTORICAL CULTURAL AND THEOLOGICAL VIEWS OF ORDER

Theologian Thomas Torrance says that three major traditions have contributed to the understanding of humankind that prevails in modern Western culture. The Greek and Roman traditions were characterized by a radical dualism of body and mind or soul, whereas the Hebrew tradition was distinctly nondualist, with body and soul forming an integrated unity. These distinctions have given rise to deep tensions, which he says we must endeavor to understand as we function in a scientific-technological culture.[2]

Greek dualism elevated the mind to almost godlike status, to a transcendent position where humans could be occupied with eternal ideas, such as truth, harmony, goodness, and beauty. Earth and its mundane sensibilities were of less consequence. The result was what Torrance calls "a persistent rationalistic disjunction of theory from practice." The Romans had a different type of dualism, one that separated body from soul by virtue of an emphasis on the material realm. The Roman mind, he points out, was intensely pragmatic, focused on the business of technical achievement, and devoted to law and order—to the respected and feared Roman justice. Rome built; its goals were an invincible army, a stable society, a strong power structure.

By contrast, the Hebrew view was a unitary one. The one God, who ruled the universe, was intimately concerned with the fortunes of his creatures. He was involved in every aspect of their society, and they were actually his earthly agents for the blessing of humankind.

As Torrance says,

It was characteristic of the Hebrew unitary view of body and soul . . . that the spiritual and the physical were not disjoined but held to be interlocked under the sustaining and holy presence of God. This is very evident, for example, in the teaching of the Old Testament about religious cleanness and uncleanness in physical life and behaviour, which is so foreign to any outlook governed by a sharp dualism of mind and body. But it is particularly evident in the conviction that God and his people were so closely bound together in the fulfilment of his supreme purpose for mankind in history, that he was not regarded as shut out of human affairs, infinitely exalted and transcendent though he is. God and his people were thought of as forming one covenanted society within the conditions of their earthly existence, while they on their part did not need to reach beyond those conditions or escape into some realm of timeless abstractions to enjoy spiritual communion with him. Integral to this Hebrew outlook was an essentially religious view of man, for human beings were regarded as related to one another and to the physical creation through the intimate presence of God and in reliance upon the constancy of his faithfulness and steadfast love. Hence, instead of religion being hived off into some arcane realm of its own, it became the inherent force affecting the way human beings regard and behave toward one another, and making for creative integration in everyday human life, thought and activity.[3]

Implied in the Hebrew conception of humankind's relationship to God was also a sense of personal relationship. God desired our love, and he also desired us to love our neighbors.

When we come to the Christian era, this sense of the personal is extended. In the Incarnation, God takes on the form of man, assumes a place of suffering and struggle alongside his creatures, and in so doing confers on his earthly Creation both reality and importance.

THE CONCEPT OF ORDER

The crucial importance of the Judeo-Christian conception of order lies in this emphasis on the transcendent God's intense interest in his creation and in his creatures. Not only was God, in the Christian view, an active participant in his world, but he had created it out of nothing, along with space and time. He was not, then, simply First Cause, and therefore part of what was made. Instead, everything that existed owed both its origin and its continuation to his creative will. Stanley Jaki, in *Cosmos and Creator,* discusses the distinctly Christian roots of the doctrine of creation out of nothing, or *creatio ex nihilo,* and attributes its first use to the theologian Tertullian (c. 200 A.D.). Its acceptance as a Christian doctrine was immediate and widespread, not only because it was consistent with the first chapter of Genesis, where the heavens and Earth have their beginning through an all-powerful God, but also because it was a necessary emphasis in confrontation with the

Hellenistic philosophy, in which the world was considered eternal and divine. Jaki says of the doctrine:

What is most telling about that declaration is its entry into Christian literature from the very beginning and the matter-of-fact manner in which that entry had been accomplished. There is no hesitation whatever on the part of those writers concerning the appropriateness of "from what was not existing" to convey the true meaning of the making of the world by Almighty God. This is certainly a striking contrast with the Greeks' attitude toward the notion of creation out of nothing. That attitude was a spontaneous dismissal, nay scorn, of the whole idea. This is why it occurs only half a dozen times in the vast corpus of classical Greek literature. . . . The Greeks of old simply could not think of a God who had a truly creative power over the universe. More often than not God, or rather the divine, was merely the noblest part of the universe. Aristotle, for one, most emphatically warned that the universe should be thought of as an orderly house but without a master, or a well-ordered army but without a commander.[4]

To get at the significance of the Judeo-Christian development in our understanding of order in the universe, we must consider the concept of contingence.

CONTINGENCE AND CONTINGENT ORDER

When events are referred to as contingent, we mean that they happen to be a certain way. In a fuller sense, however, we also imply by the word *contingent* that things do not have to be that way, and it is in this sense that the term has been applied to the Judeo-Christian concept of a universe created *ex nihilo.* Thomas Torrance deals with this application of contingence in the preface to his book *Divine and Contingent Order,* as follows:

In the history of thought this fuller sense was bound up with the Judeo-Christian conception that God freely created the universe out of nothing. This does not mean that he created it out of some stuff called "nothing," but that what he created was not created out of anything. To think of the universe as having been brought into being in this way is to hold that the universe has been given a distinctive existence of its own, utterly different from God's. We describe it as contingent for it depends on God entirely for its origin and for what it continues to be in its existence and its order. The baffling thing about the creation is that since it came into being through the free grace of God it might not have come into being at all, and now that it has come into being it contains no reason in itself why it should be what it is and why it should continue to exist. Indeed God himself was under no necessity to create the universe.[5]

The impact of this view of the creation was profound. If indeed the universe had a distinctive existence of its own, then it must also be endowed with its own authentic reality and integrity. Furthermore, its orderliness must also be contingent, being neither self-sufficient nor self-explanatory but rather having a reliability and rationality that depend upon and reflect God's own reliability and rationality. Because the universe is the free creation of an infinite God, we should not expect to be able to anticipate its character, but instead to be constantly surprised by its limitless variety of pattern and structure. As Torrance expresses it,

It is because . . . freedom and rationality within the universe are contingent upon the infinite freedom and inexhaustible rationality of God that the universe meets our inquiries with an indefinite capacity for disclosing itself to us in ways which we could not suspect, manifesting structures or patterns which we are quite unable to anticipate *a priori.* [6]

Yet our attitude toward this fascinating universe is not to be one of worship, for it is, like ourselves, a created thing. Thus our investigation into its order is wholly appropriate, as God's servants, seeking to "subdue the earth," and having "dominion" over the rest of its creatures.[7] In Donald MacKay's words, we are not an "unwelcome interloper," but rather the "servant-son at home in his Father's creation."[8] The distinctiveness of the Christian position is further brought out by R. Hooykaas in his *Religion and the Rise of Modern Science:*

The Bible knows nothing of "Nature" but knows only "creatures," who are absolutely dependent for their origin and existence on the will of God. Consequently, the natural world is admired as God's work and as evidence of its creator, but it is never adored. Nature can arouse in man a feeling of awe, but this is conquered by the knowledge that man is God's fellow-worker who shares with Him the rule of the fellow-creatures, the "dominion over the fish of the sea, and over the fowl of the air, and over the cattle, and over all the earth. . . ." Thus, in total contradiction to pagan religion, nature is not a deity to be feared and worshipped, but a work of God to be admired, studied and managed. In the Bible God and nature are no longer both opposed to man, but God and man together confront nature.[9]

Admiring God's work, then, was the fundamental basis for the scientific study of the universe. Its acceptance led, according to Torrance, to a brief period of scientific fruitfulness in the physics of space, time, light, and motion in Alexandria in the fifth and sixth centuries, but was followed by a long period of quiescence because of a resurgence of Greek ideas of causality. Still retained was the idea of the created universe as rational because its Creator and Preserver was rational, so crucial to our scientific understanding of the universe, but largely lost, was the idea of contingence. Instead, theologians preferred an emphasis upon the impassibility and immutability of God (that is, God is not subject to suffering or change), which became allied with the Aristotelian idea of God as Unmoved Mover.[10]

Historian Lynn White, Jr., provides some valuable insights into the forces operating in the medieval period that led to this narrowing of the concept of order in the universe.[11] By the year 1100 A.D., a Christian Latin theology was emerging, which placed strong emphasis upon the transcendence of the Creator. God was above all human comprehension, and his action was seen to occur, ordinarily, by means of "secondary causes," which included the agency of his creature. Because God had given humankind both intellect and freedom of will, human judgment could be a reliable resource for establishing civil law and for understanding the order of the universe. Human will and intellect were assumed, of course, to be operating within the framework of the Creator's design, but the latter's will was seen increasingly to be expressed in the form of immutable laws, the so-called laws of nature *(lex naturae)*. God orders his creation by means of these established laws, which humankind is to both comprehend and obey. Otherwise God's influence is distant and subtle. White sums up the emphasis of the medieval Latin theology:

Law, then, is inherent in God's purpose for all his creatures. It follows that he cannot be expected to tamper with it frequently in special circumstances. God is chiefly praised by the perfection with which his creatures exist according to the laws which he has established for and in them.[12]

This twelfth-century drive to stress the omnipotence of God and his underlying order was accompanied by a wave of translation of scientific works from both Greek and Arabic sources. Among these authors was Aristotle, a scholar of tremendous intellect and remarkable breadth of knowledge. Unfortunately, he was also a pagan, which led to a resurgence of ideas of an eternal world, gods and all else bound by inherent necessity, and a universe without freedom. To combat these pagan aspects of the Aristotelian system, Thomas Aquinas proceeded to reinterpret Aristotle in a way that preserved essential Christian doctrines, such as creation and personal immortality, demonstrating their logical consistency with a context ruled by human reason. This approach posed a tremendous threat to the church's concept of the absolute omnipotence of the Creator and his revelation in Scripture. As White puts it:

If sweet reason could provide so broad a foundation for Christian faith, the need for revelation was being called into question. To them the Thomistic-Aristotelian synthesis was a Trojan horse of resurgent paganism.[13]

The church, in the form of Etienne Tempier, bishop of Paris, struck back within a few years of Aquinas's death with a pronouncement of automatic excommunication for the teaching of many Aristotelian and even Thomistic propositions. It further demanded that natural philosophers start thinking about nature in non-Greek terms. The result was a revitalization of philosophical thought in the next two centuries, in which the concept of causality was greatly narrowed and a strong inclination developed toward a purely empirical examination of natural phenomena. According to Torrance, by the sixteenth and seventeenth centuries, scientists had rejected the view that in understanding the world the human mind required an antecedent set of ideas and concepts that owed nothing to experience. Instead they understood that the ideas and concepts were derivable from the world itself by empirical examination. Experiments were designed to encourage the discovery of coherent patterns that could not otherwise be known, and then these patterns were used to generate explanatory theories. Once again the stimulus for this new thrust in the scientific study of the world came as the result of a resurgence of the Christian doctrine of creation out of nothing, at the time of the Reformation. This revival reintroduced once more the concept of a universe continuously depending upon God for its reality and its order; a contingent universe.[14]

NEWTONIAN ORDER

But the new community of scientists, largely devout believers but convinced of the predominant role to be played by human reason, found a philosophical leader in Isaac Newton. He was a deeply religious man, and his conception of the relationship of God to the universe was pivotal in his thinking. According to Newton, the universe owed its rationality to the ultimate rationality and stability of God, its Creator. Yet there was, in Newton's view of God's relation to the universe, a strange inconsistency, for he saw God as unmovable and detached in his absoluteness, yet also the immanent source of the universe's precision and consistency. The latter was especially important where there were what Newton observed as irregularities in the systematic motions of the planets and stars. As Torrance points out in *Divine and Contingent Order,* this latter regulative function had unfortunate consequences for the future relationship between science and theology, for, as scientific explanations improved, the irregularities disappeared, and with them the need for the immanent Creator.[15]

Newton also addressed the question of mechanistic explanation in its relationship to the origin of the universe, emphasizing that the origin of its immanent order is not completely explainable by reference to the mechanical system itself, but depends rather upon the will and counsel of its Creator. Newton's "strangely ambiguous conception" of God's ordering activity is summed up by Torrance as follows:

On the one hand Newton's God is inertially attached to the universe in a grand synthesis which makes him through absolute time and space the supreme regulative principle by which the whole system of the world is held together, while on the other hand he is so transcendently related to the universe that he is deistically detached from it in his eternal impassibility and immutability. Through identifying absolute time with the eternal duration of God, and absolute space with the infinite presence of God, which together constitute the medium in which all things are contained, structured, and moved, Newton accounted for the natural and immutable order of the universe which operated through mechanical causes and with mathematical precision. Nevertheless, mechanical causes of that kind, Newton claimed, could not be extrapolated to account for the origin of the kind of order that obtains within the universe—for that a different kind of "cause" is required, "the agency of will." Expressed differently this means that the laws of nature do not apply to those creative processes by which what is nature came into being, but only to those observable processes of a nature that is already in being. This is a point of considerable significance, for it means, in Newton's view, that the universe cannot be conceived to be a mechanical system complete and consistent in itself, for its immanent order is not completely explainable within that system, but the universe may be conceived as a consistent mechanism if it is related to "the counsel" of a "voluntary and intelligent Agent" beyond it, the living God who rules over all.[16]

Torrance goes on to discuss the aforementioned regulative role of the Creator, and then emphasizes one primary point of Newton's system, critical for our appreciation of current views of universal order. This was his recognition that the universe is not reducible to a mechanical system, that it is not complete and consistent in itself, but requires a nonmechanical Agency to complete its intelligibility and make it accessible to scientific investigation.

MODERN SCIENCE AND THE REVIVAL OF CONTINGENT ORDER

Admittedly, it was difficult in Newton's day to appreciate the need for the immanent Creator, constantly willing the order and consistency of his creation, especially as philosophers of that time attempted to define nature with all its multivariable phenomena in terms of exclusive mechanical law. But with the advent of Einstein and his theory of special relativity, a massive shift began in the way scientists viewed the physical world.[17] Einstein demonstrated that matter and energy are related by the equation $E = mc^2$, where c is the constant and universal value for the velocity of light (of special importance, the speed of light is the same regardless of the motion of the observer), and mass is found to increase as an object's velocity approaches the speed of light. The fundamental changes for the consideration of order were that space and time were no longer separate entities, but were more correctly a single entity—space-time—and matter was seen as a form of energy. Within another decade Einstein had propounded his second great theory, general relativity. This theory dealt with gravitation, which was presented as a mathematical expression that involves the distortion of space-time. The profound implication of curved space-time was that the universe is finite, a conclusion that ultimately led to the big bang theory of the origin of the universe. Most important, where Newton had absolutized time and space, relativity theory showed time to be an intrinsic ingredient of the transformations of matter, and space was no longer seen as empty but rather filled with energy and matter. And when we come to space-time, we see a picture of what Torrance calls "a continuous, dynamic material field, with a reciprocal action between it and the constituent matter and energy of the universe, unifying and ordering everything within it."[18]

The liberating activity of Einstein's work to loose science from the Newtonian yoke is expressed by Torrance as follows:

Newton insisted on presenting the dynamic universe and interpreting continuous motion within the *idealized* framework of a geometry of relations between rigid bodies independent of time. This had the effect of clamping down upon everything in the universe a hard deterministic or mechanical structure. If that idealized Euclidean framework is dismantled, then the universe is found to manifest itself, not as a closed deterministic system, but as a continuous and open system of contingent realities and events with an inherent unifying order. As such its internal consistency must finally depend on relation to an objective ground of rationality beyond the boundaries of the contingent universe itself. That is, as I understand it, the effect of Einstein's reconstruction of classical physics: a finite but unbounded universe with open, dynamic structures grounded in a depth of objectivity and intelligibility which commands and transcends our comprehension.[19]

If Einstein's work opened the door to new and unexpected relationships between time and space, matter and energy, then the advent of quantum theory shook the very foundations of science. In Newtonian mechanics it was assumed that the description of the initial state of any system allowed an accurate prediction of its state at any future time. In the past fifty years, physics has abandoned strict causality of this kind, by virtue of the demonstration by Heisenberg that there is an element of uncertainty when we attempt to establish both position and velocity of elementary particles simultaneously. The precise orbits of planetary electrons in atoms were now seen as idealizations. In the words of Donald MacKay:

If we try to establish the exact position and speed of two atomic particles which are going to collide, we will never be able to do it accurately enough to determine exactly how they will rebound. The more exactly we observe the position, the less exactly we can specify the speed, and conversely. So the most elementary process envisaged by the mechanistic theory of classical physics—the action of one particle on another—turns out not to be precisely calculable. The cog-wheels of the classical clockwork model of the universe seem to have loose teeth! This has, of course, made a tremendous difference to the theory and practice of atomic physics. More-over, it does mean that in our present thought-model of the physical universe as a whole, absolute causality, in the sense of the unwinding of everything predictably from the initial conditions, has gone.[20]

The significance of quantum indeterminacy for our considera-tion of order is that a way is now open for chance, in its contingent sense, to interact with the laws of nature. As Polkinghorne points out, the interplay of chance and lawful necessity is the way the world develops new directions and possibilities.[21] The contingent nature of these apparently random processes is evidenced by their intelligibility and their fruitfulness. Recall his words from Chapter 3: "The universe is full of the clatter of monkeys playing with typewriters, but once they have hit on the first line of *Hamlet* it seems that they are marvellously constrained to continue to the end of at least some sort of play."[22]

But this apparent role of randomness in the fundamental work-ings of the universe has been, for many in science, a sign of emptiness and meaninglessness. Jacques Monod speaks of human-kind's aloneness "in the unfeeling vastness of the universe,"[23] and Stephen Weinberg's conclusion is that it is all pointless.[24] But, in fact, if we understand chance as contingent upon a higher intelligi-bility and rationality, we can search for and find deeper meaning and a powerful ordering structure behind the whole panorama of events in the universe. Torrance's recommendation to the scien-tific community is to be done with the "chance-necessity dialec-tic," and instead to see what appears to be accidental as coordinated with a higher kind of order.[25] Heisenberg claims that the accidental is rather more subtle than we imagine and is related to "the central order of things."[26] Torrance goes on to suggest that we also take a "trajectory of temporal motion into our basic equa-tions" in order to comprehend the cohesion of contingent events.[27] The latter would be especially valuable in our understanding of the remarkable unidirectional processes of the universe, including evolutionary directions in living systems and in the expanding cosmos.

Indeed, it is recent developments in research on these nonlinear processes that lead to a new appreciation of the depth and power of ordering forces in the universe.

RECENT DEVELOPMENTS POINTING TO DEEP AND POWERFUL ORDERING FORCES

THERMODYNAMICS OF FAR-FROM-EQUILIBRIUM SYSTEMS

Order Through Fluctuations

Belgian Nobel laureate Ilya Prigogine tells us, in his book *Order Out of Chaos*, written with Isabelle Stengers,[28] that the science of thermodynamics brought with it a new concept of time as unidirectional. The mechanistic worldview that dominated Western science from the time of Newton had sought to organize nature into all-inclusive schemes, universal frameworks in which all the parts were logically or causally interconnected. There were to be no gaps left open for spontaneous, unexpected events that were not explicable on the basis of the immutable laws of nature. But by the middle of the nineteenth century, scientists were introducing new concepts that had to do with heat engines and energy conversion, and the science of thermodynamics was born. One of its key components was the second law, which introduced the idea of disorder, or entropy, and explained the frequently observed inefficiency associated with energy conversion. In these cases some of the energy had been converted to an unusable form represented by the increased molecular disorder of the system. The implication of the second law was far-reaching; there was an irreversible direction to natural processes. Time had an arrow, and it pointed in the direction of an inescapable loss of energy in the universe. The new thermodynamic ideas about a direction in natural processes were foreign to the machine-minded, who saw the universe as clockwork: the planets timelessly orbited the sun, and all systems equilibrated and operated in a deterministic fashion. The response of the mechanists was to regard the irreversible processes with which thermodynamics was concerned as rare and inconsequential.

But Prigogine's thesis is that irreversible processes are in fact the predominant kind, and classical mechanics succeeds only as it idealizes otherwise irreversible processes by ignoring friction and other limiting features. And, of utmost importance, in moving from the reversible, equilibrium situation to the irreversible, far-from-equilibrium one, a whole new character of natural processes is revealed, and a new kind of order appears. Examples of these ordering processes come readily to mind. The flow of water from a faucet goes through a series of ordered structures as the flow rate is changed. Superconductivity in metals at certain low temperatures reveals a collective ordering of electrons. And living systems reveal a high level of order in far-from-equilibrium conditions. One of the most fascinating visual effects is seen in a chemical phenomenon called the Belousov-Zhabotinsky reaction. When malonic acid, bromate, and cerium ions are placed in sulfuric acid in a shallow dish at certain critical temperatures, a series of pulsating concentric and spiral circles develop, almost as if they were life forms. This behavior is the result of giant oscillations of millions of molecules, operating in concert, in the reaction system. The key feature of this kind of chemical phenomenon is the presence of autocatalysis: one or more of the reacting species is able to catalyze its own synthesis, and the whole system seems to pivot on this autocatalytic step. In contrast to chemical reactions in which reagents and products are distributed randomly in the solution, in the Belousov-Zhabotinsky type of reaction there are local inhomogeneities; in one region, one component may predominate, while in another part of the reaction vessel its concentration may be exhausted. The cooperative effect of a vast number of such reactant molecules leads to the pulsating, highly ordered arrangements. It is Prigogine's thesis that these structures are the inevitable consequences of far-from-equilibrium reactions. The term he uses for this phenomenon is "order through fluctuation."

A simpler type of far-from-equilibrium chemical system is the chemical clock, studied by Prigogine and his collaborators by means of a model which he refers to as a "Brusselator." The model is distinguished by another kind of catalytic feature, "crosscatalysis," in which two components reciprocally affect each other's synthesis. The fluctuations in this model system are found to be of a highly specific periodicity, reflected in a remarkable change in composition, from all of one component to all of a second component, practically instantaneously. Here we have an example of oscillations in time. In the Belousov-Zhabotinsky reaction the oscillations are both time- and space-dependent, with waves of the two predominant species of molecules passing periodically through the system.

Another instance of order through fluctuations, this time in a physical system, is the Bernard instability, in which one heats a liquid layer from the bottom and thereby establishes a temperature gradient from bottom to top. At low temperature differences heat is transferred by conduction, and the fluid as a whole remains at rest. But at some critical temperature value, a convection current appears spontaneously, and a huge cooperative movement of the molecules of the liquid occurs, which takes the form of a grid of hexagonal cells. Prigogine emphasizes that according to the laws of statistics the original microscopic convection current should have been doomed to regression. Instead the minute fluctuation is amplified until it invades the entire system. As Prigogine expresses it, "Beyond the critical value of the imposed gradient, a new molecular order has been produced spontaneously. It corresponds to a giant fluctuation stabilized through energy exchanges with the outside world."[29]

The Living System

If nonlinear autocatalytic reactions are uncommon in the inorganic world, they are the rule when you examine the metabolic processes of the living system. The characteristic of living things is homeostasis, the maintenance of an ordered flow of energy to the cells and tissues of the organism and a conversion of that energy into structure and function. The metabolic pathways of the thousands of components involved are regulated by feedback loops and crosscatalytic steps similar to those of chemical clocks.

Prigogine notes a distinction between the inorganic and the biological: the existence of complexity in the reaction mechanism in the former and complexity in the reacting molecules (the proteins, nucleic acids, and so on) in the latter. This he attributes to the uniqueness of the biological system in having a past: the complex biomolecules are a product of evolutionary selection to perform a highly specific function.[30]

Prigogine goes on to illustrate the extent to which metabolic processes in living systems demonstrate the character of fluctuating, self-ordering systems. For this he uses the well-characterized process of glycolysis, the fundamental energy-producing cycle during which the sugar glucose is broken down through a series of metabolic reactions to yield the energy-rich substance ATP (adenosine triphosphate). Each glucose molecule degraded leads to the conversion of two molecules of ADP (adenosine diphosphate) into ATP, and the ATP is recycled into ADP as its high energy is utilized in metabolism. This metabolic sequence displays oscillatory behavior, and its rate-controlling steps operate at far-from-equilibrium conditions. In Prigogine's words,

Biochemical experiments have discovered the existence of temporal oscillations in concentrations related to the glycolytic cycle. It has been shown that these oscillations are determined by a key step in the reaction sequence, a step activated by ADP and inhibited by ATP. This is a typical nonlinear phenomenon well suited to regulate metabolic functioning. Indeed, each time the cell draws on its energy reserves, it is exploiting the phosphate bonds, and ATP is converted into ADP. ADP accumulation inside the cell thus signifies intensive energy consumption and the need to replenish stocks. ATP accumulation, on the other hand, means that glucose can be broken down at a slower rate.

Theoretical investigation of this process has shown that this mechanism is indeed liable to produce an oscillation phenomenon, a chemical clock. The theoretically calculated values of the chemical concentrations necessary to produce oscillation and the period of the cycle agree with the experimental data. Glycolytic oscillation produces a modulation of all the cell's energy processes which are dependent on ATP concentration and therefore indirectly on numerous other metabolic chains.

We may go farther and show that in the glycolytic pathway the reactions controlled by some of the key enzymes are in far-from-equilibrium conditions. Such calculations have been reported by Benno Hess and have since been extended to other systems. Under usual conditions the glycolytic cycle corresponds to a chemical clock, but changing these conditions can induce spatial pattern formations in complete agreement with the predictions of existing theoretical models.[31]

Prigogine and his coworkers also examine the complex aggregation behavior of the slime mold *Dictyostelium discoideum.* Depending upon the nutritional state of the environment, the unicellular amoebae can grow and migrate as free-swimming organisms, or, under starvation conditions, undergo a spectacular transformation in which several thousand cells aggregate to form a footlike structure that provides support for a mass of spores. Prigogine describes the first stage of the aggregation process as beginning with the onset of displacement waves in the population of amoebae, directed toward a center of attraction that appears to be produced spontaneously. This migration of cells appears to be in response to a gradient of the biochemical messenger, cycle AMP, first produced by the cell that forms the attractor center. Here again we see the characteristics of a chemical clock, but here, in this simple differentiation phenomenon, the self-organization mechanism actually leads to communication between the cells. Indeed, one of the hallmarks of these self-organizing systems seems to be their coherence. The individuals involved behave as a unit, as if their movement was the result of long-range forces. Yet preceding these ordering processes there is an inherent instability, as if each system was composed of subsystems that were constantly fluctuating. These fluctuations, when powerful enough and timed properly, can shatter the preexisting organization and lead to the new level of organization. Prigogine emphasizes that the point of change, the bifurcation point, is unpredictable; it is indeterminate in the philosophical sense. But it is also unpredictable in direction—whether the transition will be to chaotic behavior or to a new, higher level of order.

It is tempting to apply these characteristics of the self-organizing system to the origin of life. Prigogine and Nicholis have suggested that biogenesis may have occurred by just such a progression of events, with simple self-organizing chemical systems reaching points of bifurcation, then, by virtue of available energy, moving to progressively higher forms of complexity and finally to the first primitive cell. In their words, "One would then obtain a hierarchy of dissipative structures, each one enriched further by the information content of the previous models through the 'memory' of the initial fluctuations which created them successively."[32] Arthur Peacocke's excitement about this possible route to life is apparent when he says,

> Because of the discovery of these dissipative systems, and of the possibility of "order-through fluctuations," it is now possible, on the basis of these physicochemical considerations, to regard as highly probable the emergence of those ordered and articulated molecular structures which are living. Instead of them having only an inconceivably small chance of emerging in the "primeval soup" on the surface of the earth before life appeared, we now see that ordered dissipative structures of some kind will appear in due course. To this extent, the emergence of life was inevitable, but the form it was to take remained entirely open and unpredictable, at least to us.[33]

We seem now to be back to the picture of a contingent order, built into the stuff of life by the Creator. The living system remains unpredictable by virtue of its sheer complexity but also because an openness, a multiplicity of bifurcation points, appears to be inherent in its origin and in its operation.

Universal Constants in Chaotic Behavior

Mathematical analysis of nonlinear phenomena has proved difficult. The usual approach to these many and varied systems is to simplify them to approximate a linear situation. Arthur Fisher, in an article in *Mosaic,* quotes a graduate student at Los Alamos National Laboratory's Center for Nonlinear Studies as saying,

> "Your textbook is full of linear problems, and you become adept at solving them. When you're confronted with a nonlinear problem, you're

taught immediately to linearize it; you make an approximation, use a special case. But when you venture into the real world, you realize that many problems are non-linear in an essential way and cannot be linearized meaningfully. You would just lose the physics."[34]

One of the most fascinating studies of nonlinear phenomena is that of Mitchell Feigenbaum, who has found that only a limited number of patterns lead to chaotic behavior. That is to say, transitions to chaos are ordered. One of these patterns is called period doubling, the process by which the periodic behavior of a system falters and becomes erratic as a particular parameter, for example, temperature, is changed. In the usual periodic process there is a fixed time interval between repetitions. As some parameter is changed, this interval does not change gradually or randomly, but doubles at each change. And the process of successive doubling is found to recur continually, until at a certain value of the parameter under change, in Feigenbaum's words, "it has doubled ad infinitum, so that the behavior is no longer periodic." Chaos has set in, but by a precise route of period doubling.

Judging from the results obtained in this new science of chaotic behavior, it seems that there may be subtle yet powerful forces of order throughout nature. And the expectation is that there is more evidence of this to come. As one of the "chaos scientists," David Ruelle, says, "There is a whole world of forms still to be explored and harmonies still to be discovered."[35]

ORDER AS WHOLENESS

In a recent book entitled *Looking Glass Universe: The Emerging Science of Wholeness,* authors John Briggs and David Peat present the work of a number of scientists who are convinced that studying the world by disassembling it into parts leads to significant distortion.[36] Physicist David Bohm insists that some of science's most popular ideas lead to erroneous conclusions. For example, Bohm points out that the opposite of order is popularly thought to be disorder, or randomness. Instead, what appears as disorder may be a condition of a higher degree of order. An example is the puzzling double-slit experiment.[37] Electrons are considered elementary particles, and photons are considered single indivisible quanta of energy. When a stream of photons is fired at a target with two slits in it, the photons interfere with each other and form an overlapping wave pattern on a screen behind them. The same result is obtained if a stream of electrons is fired at the target. And if photons or electrons are fired at the target one by one, you would expect that, in the absence of interference, a simple scatter pattern would be observed behind each of the slits. Instead a wave pattern is still obtained, as if all of the electrons had been fired at the same time! Explanations for this phenomenon seem desperate. One suggestion is that each individual electron goes through both slits and interferes with itself. A second approach proposes that each particle is aware of the fate of its predecessors and successors, and it is the aggregate of these "awarenesses" that leads to the wave pattern on the screen. Quantum physicists, rejecting both ideas, simply conclude that the laws of physics don't apply to individual particles or quanta—only to large numbers, where the rules of probability apply. For David Bohm, the result of the double-slit experiment suggests that a high degree of order exists where we previously thought we were dealing with the random behavior of individual particles. It is consistent with a picture of a whole, or unbroken, universe, in which there is no separation into parts that are ordered and parts that are disordered.

A second example of wholeness is seen in the strange behavior of elementary particles studied in high-voltage accelerators.[38] When protons are smashed in an accelerator, they divide into a number of other particles, but after several rapid transitions they return to the form of the original proton. To use Briggs and Peat's term, they "divide back into themselves." A similar behavior is observed when quarks, the presumed fundamental particles, are split away from mesons. The freed quarks immediately recombine to form new mesons. The quantum mechanical picture is that of a wholeness that can't be divided.

Bohm's "science of undivided wholeness," as Briggs and Peat explain it, is best described by analogy to the hologram. Whereas an ordinary photograph is really an abstraction, a mapping of certain aspects of three-dimensional reality onto a two-dimensional form, thereby dividing the scene into parts, the hologram is a composite of the entire three-dimensional scene. This is because the holographic image is constructed by directing a laser beam (light of uniform phase) through a holographic plate on which a scene has been recorded in a special manner. By means of a half-silvered mirror, laser light is split into two beams, one to illuminate the object and the other to act as a kind of reference beam. The light striking the object is scattered, and is recorded on the plate as a mixture of phases, much like sound from a stereo set. The reference beam, by comparison, contains light all in one phase. The mixing of the two beams at the plate results in an interference pattern. Briggs and Peat say the result is a "very fine pattern of light and dark patches, a kind of code."[39]

With this interference pattern recorded on a photographic plate it is possible to produce a holographic image by shining laser light through the plate and projecting the pattern on a screen. The image produced appears three-dimensional, and the plate itself contains a record of the reference and scattered beams. The fascinating thing about the holographic record is that every part of the plate contains the whole image. If you tear off a piece of an ordinary photographic negative, it contains only a piece of the original picture. But if a piece of a holographic plate is torn off, projection of a laser beam through the fragment gives the whole image, though with diminished crispness.

David Bohm sees the hologram as an analogy for the undivided order of the universe, a frozen version of what is occurring on an infinitely vaster scale all over the universe. He sees the universe as a vast array of light waves and other electromagnetic radiations, constantly interacting with each other and with matter, generating interference patterns that are ever-changing and evolving, recording incalculable amounts of information about the objects and events encountered. Within the record you would expect to find information about an object's geometry, internal structure, and perhaps even the nature of its change with time. Bohm's idea is that these interactions occur even at the subatomic level, where elementary particles, also describable as wave patterns, are capable of interaction with the external wave forms.

As Briggs and Peat describe it,

Remember that matter is also waves. Therefore the very matter of objects is itself composed of interference patterns which interfere with the patterns of energy. What emerges is a picture of an encoding pattern of matter and energy spreading ceaselessly throughout the universe—each region of space, no matter how small (all the way down to the single photon, which is also a wave or "wave packet"), containing—as does each region of the holographic plate—the pattern of the whole, including all the past and with implications for all the future. Each region will carry this encoding of the whole somewhat differently, as in fact different "parts" of a holographic plate will each give the whole picture but with slightly different limitations on the number of perspectives from which it can be seen.

It is a breathtaking view, an infinite holographic universe where each region is a distinct perspective, yet each contains all. . . . Everything mirrors everything else; the universe is a looking-glass.[40]

In David Bohm's words in his book *Wholeness and the Implicate Order:*

There is the germ of a new notion of order here. This order is not to be understood solely in terms of a regular arrangement of objects (e.g., in rows) or as a regular arrangement of events (e.g., in a series). Rather, a total order is contained, in some implicit sense, in each region of space and time.

Now, the word "implicit" is based on the verb "to implicate." This means "to fold inward" (as multiplication means "folding many times"). So we may be led to explore the notion that in some sense each region contains a total structure "enfolded" within it.[41]

THEOLOGICAL CORRELATES TO NEW CONCEPTS OF ORDER

The pioneers of science marched to the frontier with the conviction that God had created a rational and ordered universe, one that would answer their inquiries rationally, if sometimes surprisingly.

Then, too, it was to be enjoyed, to be of benefit, but not to be worshiped, for it was only a creature. But as a creature the universe had an order and an authentic reality that was contingent, being neither self-sufficient nor self-explanatory, but depending upon and reflecting God's own reliability and rationality.

By the late medieval period, the concept of order was narrowed, to place major emphasis on God's transcendence. God's order was seen to be expressed in the form of natural laws, and human reason had to discern these fixed rules of the universe. By the sixteenth century the valid means of discernment had been established as empirical examination, followed by the testing of explanatory theories. By the time of Isaac Newton, the universe was largely seen as clockwork, with God as clockmaker and occasional adjuster, but largely distant from his creation. What was largely lost in this somewhat static view of order was the concept of the universe as contingent.

Revival of the concept of contingent order has come with the advent of modern relativity and quantum theory. Space and time are understood not to be absolute and, in fact, are seen as inseparable. Furthermore, space-time is curved, and the universe is therefore finite. Quantum theory and Heisenberg's uncertainty principle have eliminated strict causality, opening the way for contingent order, for chance to interact with the fixed laws of nature. Chance events have taken on a deep theological meaning, for they may properly be seen as the expressed will of the Creator of a higher kind of order. Hints of the nature of this order come from the work of Ilya Prigogine on far-from-equilibrium systems. Prigogine stresses the preponderance of these nonlinear processes in the universe, their characteristic instability and unpredictability, but the surprising degree to which perturbations lead to higher and more complex levels of order. In the course of these transitions, large groups of molecules function as units, suggesting a high degree of intermolecular communication. The same type of behavior seems to be characteristic of living systems, and provides a framework to explain their origin. Feigenbaum's work on period doubling of nonlinear systems also emphasizes the extent of ordering processes in the universe, for even in transitions from order to apparently random behavior, systems follow specific prescribed routes. So, whether perturbation of a far-from-equilibrium system leads to a higher level of order or to chaotic behavior, the transitions are themselves ordered. Indeed, there appear to be deep and profound ordering forces at work in all natural processes.

Similarly, the implications of Bohm's view of wholeness for a deeper understanding of order in the universe are profound. It would seem appropriate to explore theological correlates in dealing with this picture of order, this seamless enfolding, in which not only matter and energy but also space and time are brought together in one vast hologram of the universe.

Such a construct demands something or someone even greater as its mediator, and it is intriguing to recall the biblical description of the immanent Creator Jesus Christ, God's Son, given in the letter to the Hebrews: "He reflects the glory of God and bears the very stamp of his nature, upholding the universe by his word of power."[42]

Donald MacKay tells us, in his *Science and Christian Faith Today*,[43] that we may think of the last phrase, "upholding the universe by his word of power," as *"holding in being* the universe by his word of power." This distinction allows us to rid ourselves of the image of God as only a machine-tender or caretaker, and gives us instead the picture of an immanent Creator, whose involvement with his vast creation every moment ensures its very existence as well as its order. The extent of the Creator's power and the sense of his presence at every level of the created order is awesome. And by this order he brings coherence and rationality to make intelligible what would otherwise be baffling. It is as though the scientific history of our world was like a great musical masterpiece composed for our ears. Indeed, Arthur R. Peacocke makes just such an analogy when he writes of God's music of creation:

He is more like a composer who, beginning with an arrangement of notes in an apparently simple tune, elaborates and expands it into a fugue by a variety of devices of fragmentation and reassociation; of turning it upside down and back to front; by overlapping these and other variations of it in a range of tonalities; by a profusion of patterns of sequences in time, with always the consequent interplay of sound flowing in an orderly way from the chosen initiating ploy (that is more technically, by inversion, stretto, and canon, etc.). Thus does a J. S. Bach create a complex and interlocking harmonious fusion of his seminal material, both through time and at any particular instant, which, beautiful in its elaboration, only reaches its consummation when all the threads have been drawn into the return to the home key of the last few bars—the key of the initial melody whose potential elaboration was conceived from the moment it was first expounded.[44]

NOTES

1. Col. 1:15; Heb. 1:3, RSV.
2. Thomas F. Torrance, *The Christian Frame of Mind* (Edinburgh: Handsel Press, 1985), 29.
3. Ibid., 30.
4. Stanley L. Jaki, *Cosmos and Creator* (Chicago: Gateway Editions, 1980), 72–73.
5. Thomas F. Torrance, *Divine and Contingent Order* (Oxford: Oxford University Press, 1981), vii.
6. Ibid., 22.
7. Gen. 1:26, 28, RSV.
8. Donald M. MacKay, "Biblical Perspectives on Human Engineering," in *Modifying Man: Implications and Ethics,* ed. Craig Ellison (Washington, D.C.: University Press of America, 1978).
9. R. Hooykaas, *Religion and the Rise of Modern Science* (Grand Rapids: Eerdmans, 1972), 8, 9.
10. Torrance, *Divine and Contingent Order,* 4–6.
11. Lynn White, Jr., "Science and the Sense of Self," in *Limits of Scientific Inquiry,* ed. G. Holton and R. S. Morison (New York: W. W. Norton, 1979), 47–59.
12. Ibid., 48.
13. Ibid., 50.
14. Thomas F. Torrance, "Theological and Scientific Inquiry," *Journal of the American Scientific Affiliation* 2 (1986): 38.
15. Torrance, *Divine and Contingent Order,* 8–10.
16. Ibid., 10.
17. Iain Paul, *Science, Theology and Einstein* (New York: Oxford University Press, 1982).
18. Torrance, *Divine and Contingent Order,* 13.
19. Ibid., 11.
20. Donald M. MacKay, *The Clockwork Image* (Downers Grove, IL: InterVarsity Press, 1974), 14–15.
21. John Polkinghorne, *The Way the World Is* (Grand Rapids: Eerdmans, 1983), 22.

22. Ibid., 11.
23. Jacques Monod, *Chance and Necessity* (New York: Vantage Books, 1972).
24. Steven Weinberg, *The First Three Minutes* (New York: Bantam Books, 1977), 144.
25. Torrance, *Divine and Contingent Order*, 47–48.
26. Werner Heisenberg, *Physics and Beyond* (New York: Harper & Row, 1971), 84, 214ff., 241, 243, 247.
27. Torrance, *Divine and Contingent Order*, 47.
28. Ilya Prigogine and Isabelle Stengers, *Order Out of Chaos* (New York: Bantam Books, 1984).
29. Ibid., 143.
30. Ibid., 153.
31. Ibid., 155.
32. Ilya Prigogine and G. Nicolis, *Quarterly Review of Biophysics* 4 (1971): 132.
33. Arthur R. Peacocke, *Creation and the World of Science* (Oxford: Clarendon Press, 1979), 100.
34. Arthur Fisher, "Chaos, the Ultimate Asymmetry," *Mosaic* 16 (Jan./Feb. 1985): 26.
35. Ibid., 33.
36. John P. Briggs and F. David Peat, *Looking Glass Universe: The Emerging Science of Wholeness* (New York: Simon and Schuster, 1984). p 51–53
37. Ibid., 51–52.
38. Ibid., 77–78.
39. Ibid., 108–112.
40. Ibid., 111–12.
41. David Bohm, *Wholeness and the Implicate Order* (London: Routledge and Kegan Paul, 1980), 149.
42. Heb. 1:3, RVS.
43. Donald M. MacKay, *Science and Christian Faith Today* (London: CPAS Publications, 1973), 8.
44. Peacocke, *Creation and Science*, 107.

7. The Vast Arena of Faith

THE PERVASIVE BELIEF IN A HIGHER LAW OF CONDUCT

One of the most perceptive writers of our century is C. S. Lewis, Oxford don and Cambridge professor. In his book *Mere Christianity,* Lewis opens his arguments for the Christian faith with a discussion of right and wrong as a clue to the meaning of the universe. He observes that we all, in our human relationships, operate as though there were common standards of right and wrong. Furthermore, this is a universal phenomenon common to the ancient Egyptians, Babylonians, Hindus, Chinese, Greeks, and Romans, and our own present-day culture. Differences in degree occur at certain points, but all agree that, for example, selfishness should never be admired. Second, he notes that we all have in common the recognition that our standards are higher than we can achieve. We all accept the fact, in the way we react to our standards, that we should do better, even if we don't want to. Of course we often have good excuses. In fact, they come so quickly and in such profusion that they are, Lewis says, a proof of how deeply we believe in right and wrong, or in what he calls the law of human nature. Concerning these two points, Lewis concludes,

First, that human beings, all over the earth, have this curious idea that they ought to behave in a certain way, and cannot really get rid of it. Secondly, that they don't in fact behave in that way. They know the Law of Nature; they break it. These two facts are the foundation of all clear thinking about ourselves and the universe we live in.[1]

Now what is most interesting about right and wrong is that the small differences in moral code between cultures are distinguishable in a way that allows us to speak of moral progress. That is, some civilizations have achieved a higher moral code than others.

But the moment you admit that one set of moral ideas is superior to another, you are, in fact, measuring them both by a standard, saying that one conforms to that standard better than the other. The logical conclusion, then, is that there must exist some universal, absolute standard to which all of our moral concepts relate.

Furthermore, this absolute standard, this law of human nature, is distinct from natural laws dealing with things such as gravity or heredity or chemistry. For there is no sense in which we can disobey the law of gravity, but there is overwhelming evidence that we can, and do, break the law of human nature. Lewis concludes,

Men ought to be unselfish, ought to be fair. Not that men are unselfish, nor that they like being unselfish, but that they ought to be. The Moral Law, or Law of Human Nature, is not simply a fact about human behaviour in the same way as the Law of Gravitation is, or may be, simply a fact about how heavy objects behave. On the other hand, it is not a mere fancy, for we cannot get rid of the idea, and most of the things we say and think about men would be reduced to nonsense if we did. And it is not simply a statement about how we should like men to behave for our own convenience; for the behaviour we call bad or unfair is not exactly the same as the behavior we find inconvenient, and may even be the opposite. Consequently, this Rule of Right and Wrong, or Law of Human Nature, or whatever you call it, must somehow or other be a real thing—a thing that is really there, not made up by ourselves. And yet it is not a fact in the ordinary sense, in the same way as our actual behaviour is a fact. It begins to look as if we shall have to admit that there is more than one kind of reality; that, in this particular case, there is something above and beyond the ordinary facts of men's behaviour, and yet quite definitely real—a real law, which none of us made, but which we find pressing on us.[2]

This phenomenon of universal moral sense is also recognized by the mathematical physicist John Polkinghorne in his book *The Way the World Is.* He notes that there is within us a remarkable sense of hope, in the face of a world of mixed goodness and terror. It is a sense that derives ultimately from our faith in a Transcendent Power.[3] In our age voices have explained away these feelings as mere superstitions from a bygone era when the theistic view was almost universal. But their validity as transcendent experience is argued for from a variety of sociological standpoints. Sociologist Peter Berger, in his book *A Rumor of Angels,* introduces five phenomena, or "signals of transcendence," that serve as pointers toward a religious explanation of human behavior.[4] One of these is the human faith in order, a faith closely related to humankind's fundamental trust of reality. The example he gives is of a young child awaking in the night crying, perhaps because of a bad dream. His mother goes to him to give comfort and reassurance, taking him in her arms, lighting the lamp, and saying words such as, "Don't be afraid. It's all right." But of course we know, in a world of cancer and famine and terrorism, all is not right. Is this, then, a monstrous deception? Of course not. It is the appropriate behavior, which we all would encourage. It is appropriate because we believe in the religious dimension. We believe that there is an Order in the affairs of humankind, a Power that ultimately is concerned for our good. In Berger's words,

In the observable human propensity to order reality there is an intrinsic impulse to give cosmic scope to this order, an impulse that implies not only that human order in some way corresponds to an order that transcends it, but that this transcendent order is of such a character that man can trust himself and his destiny to it. There is a variety of human roles that represent this conception of order, but the most fundamental is the parental role. Every parent (or, at any rate, every parent who loves his child) takes upon himself the representation of a universe that is ultimately in order and ultimately trustworthy. This representation can be justified only within a religious (strictly speaking, a supernatural) frame of reference. In this frame of reference the natural world within which we are born, love, and die is not the only world, but only the foreground of another world in which love is not annihilated in death, and in which, therefore, the trust in the power of love to banish chaos is justified. Thus man's ordering propensity implies a transcendent order, and each ordering gesture is a signal of this transcendence. The parental role is not based on a loving lie. On the contrary, it is a witness to the ultimate truth of man's situation in reality. In that case, it is perfectly possible (even, if one is so inclined, in Freudian terms) to analyze religion as a cosmic projection of the child's experience of the protective order of parental love. What is projected is, however, itself a reflection, an imitation, of ultimate reality. Religion, then, is not only (from the point of view of empirical reason) a projection of human order, but (from the point of view of what might be called inductive faith) the ultimately true vindication of human order.[5]

THE BREADTH OF RELIGIOUS EXPERIENCE IN MODERN CULTURE

Among significant scientific contributors to our understanding of modern religious experience, the late Sir Alistair Hardy, Oxford marine biologist and ecologist, stands almost without peer. Social anthropologists had worked with a variety of primitive tribes for the preceding twenty years, and some, such as Edward Evans-Pritchard, had reported remarkable accounts of spiritual awareness among primitive communities.[6] And psychologist William James, in his pioneering study of religious feeling, *The Varieties of Religious Experience,* written in 1902, had presented an earlier view of the religious impulse, especially in the context of evangelical Protestant Christianity.[7] But only Hardy researched the question of religious experience in the broad sweep of contemporary British society, and in a period when most of his scientific peers were reductionists, who regarded religious feelings as by-products of the brain's chemical processes. Hardy was convinced of the importance and reality of spiritual experience throughout his career as a biologist. By the time he achieved the position of president of the Zoology Section of the British Association, in 1949, he publicly expressed his dissatisfaction with the tendency of his colleagues to reduce all of biology to materialistic, mechanistic explanation.

In 1965 he published *The Living Stream,* a reexamination of evolutionary theory, which proposed a stronger contribution by human consciousness and acquired knowledge in human evolution.[8] Intrinsic to this process, and perhaps foundational to it, is the religious dimension. Like one of his contemporaries, Michael Polanyi,

Alistair Hardy believed that science and religion had much to offer each other. He spoke of the goal of a "scientific theology"—a natural theology—which would enlighten us about the place of Divine Power in human affairs. And he pointed out to his contemporaries that the history of science demonstrated the importance of that goal. In his words,

The whole history of science has been a direct search for God, deliberate and conscious, until well into the eighteenth century. . . . Copernicus, Kepler, Galileo, Newton, Leibnitz and the rest did not merely believe in God in an orthodox sort of way: they believed that their work told humanity more about God than had been known before. Their incentive in working at all was a desire to know God; and they regarded their discoveries as not only proving his existence, but as revealing more and more of his nature.[9]

What was needed, Hardy said, was an extensive natural history of religion. And so, in 1969, he founded the Religious Experience Research Unit at Manchester College. In the ensuing years he compiled and classified data on religious experiences in Britain and concluded, on ecological analysis of eighteen hundred firsthand accounts, that 30 percent of that country's population had had a significant religious experience. Furthermore, the experience was not limited to the uneducated or unsophisticated: more than 56 percent of the better educated gave similar reports. His conclusion, set forth in part in a 1979 book, *The Spiritual Nature of Man,* is that religion is something deeply rooted in human nature but stifled and repressed by the materialism of our day.[10] According to him, religious experience is an essential component of human consciousness, an intrinsic part of the evolutionary origin of humankind. Hardy says, "The living stream of evolution is as much Divine as physical in nature."[11]

In the final pages of *The Living Stream,* Hardy turns his focus to his colleagues in biology who still fail to see the significance of the spiritual in all of experience. He looks to a new era of exploration, to a "truer biology," which "will not sell its soul to physics and chemistry for quick results." The fields yet to conquer are challenging indeed. He mentions consciousness, memory, feelings of purpose and joy, the sense of the sacred, the sense of right and wrong, and the appreciation of beauty.[12] And we are left with the feeling that, on that basis, we have barely begun our science, so great is the breadth of spiritual experience.

SCIENCE OPENS A VAST FRAMEWORK OF BELIEF

THE BEGINNINGS OF SCIENCE

Not only is faith a common element in the experience of different nationalities and cultures throughout history, and of a cross-section of economic and educational groups in contemporary society, but it has a profound involvement in the practice of science. Indeed, the beginnings of science were earmarked by an almost complete solidarity of religious conviction among its practitioners. Furthermore, their convictions were characterized by a heightened level of spiritual insight and an appreciation of God's creation so extraordinary that their fledgling discipline brought about the scientific revolution.

The reason for the success of the scientific enterprise was, in the view of philosopher-scientist Walter Thorson, traceable to these theological roots.[13] Scientists were taking God's creation seriously, in a way foreign to the medieval church. The truth about the physical world was not only fascinating to explore but, in the view of these devout people, a valid description of a genuine reality. If theologians of the period regarded the physical world as only a kind of papier-mâché stage prop for the playing out of the drama of salvation, believing scientists saw it instead as a valid source of blessing with its own integrity and spiritual opportunity. Here was a place to be explored in an effort to fully appreciate the Divine Artist's handiwork.

The historical roots of the scientific revolution lie in the philosophical tradition of nominalism, which stressed openness to divine revelation and took exception to the competing philosophy of rationalism. The major point of contention was that rationalists raised human reason to the level of absolute truth and spoke of the a priori necessity of rational order. The nominalists argued that there is no necessary rational order in the universe; it is as it happens to be. That is, it is contingent, subject to the will of the Creator. The forms reason gives to our study of the world are conveniences, which at best agree with reality and at worst are inventions of our minds. R. Hooykaas, in his *Religion and the Rise of Modern Science*, points out that, with the exception of Descartes and one or two others, all the early scientists embraced the nominalist view.[14] Apparently these Christians saw in nominalism an encouragement for their science, but in rationalism they saw instead obstruction. Walter Thorson explains the situation as follows:

First, these early scientists emphasized their appreciation of the intellectual humility and openness of the nominalist view—and contrasted it with the arrogance of rationalism as they had encountered it. They stressed the idea that rationalism fosters pride and an overconfident dogmatism, and they never tired of pointing out that this produces both error and a closed mind. Francis Bacon epitomized this attitude when he insisted that if a man wishes to know reality, he must abandon the dogmatic confidence of his pride in reason alone and sit down humbly before the revelation of God, whether that were the book of Scripture or the book of nature. This parallel between scientific and religious knowledge, both of which are to be acquired by "reading the revelation of God," and not by *a priori* reason, is a favorite and important emphasis of the early scientists. The parallel has been deliberately ignored by secular accounts of the scientific revolution, which identify empiricism, i.e., sense experience, as the important ingredient. Professor Hooykaas shows us that for the early scientists the relevant issue is not empiricism per se, but the nominalist tradition, which emphasized contact with reality itself as the only source of truth. These early thinkers thought of themselves as "empiricists" with respect to Scripture as well as with respect to creation. It is an attitude we need to examine deeply if we claim to believe in revelation.

The second attitude which appears to have been fostered by this nominalism of early scientists entails, not a complete rejection of the validity of reason, but its acceptance as a useful tool of the human mind. As I mentioned, earlier thrusts of nominalism had sometimes denied all validity to abstract reasoning; this new nominalism retains reason, but gives it a human place, not a divine one. It is a useful skill, like our perceptive skills, but it must not be made into an absolute, and it must be educated by constant encounter with reality. The importance and fruitfulness of this attitude cannot possibly be over-estimated.

Third, and partly as a result of the first two attitudes, this nominalism creates or heightens the distinction between truth as an objective reality, existing independently and outside myself, and my knowledge of the truth, which involves the interpretation, by my reason, of my experience of that reality. This was important for the early scientists, who were keenly aware that they had much to learn before they could competently think the Creator's thoughts after Him. They clearly saw that the main mistake of rationalist thought is to confuse the rational representation of truth with truth itself, and they understood that this mistake fosters dogmatism and pride.[15]

FAITH LOST: THE RISE OF MODERN PHILOSOPHY

If the faith of the pioneers of science was such a motivating force for the scientific revolution, why did faith lose its power as the prime mover of science only a few centuries later? Most philosophers would identify the mathematician Descartes as the originator of the modern scientific philosophical tradition, a tradition that claimed as its central tenet the autonomy of the human mind. In this Descartes did not deny the existence of divine revelation, but what he did deny was the idea that philosophy could rest upon commitments to presuppositions and ideas derived from revelation. As Thorson describes the role of Descartes,

He defined the task of philosophy as the establishment of an intelligible knowledge of the world without presupposing any religious or personal beliefs. The ground for doing so he took to be the knower himself, and from this ground he proposed not only to derive all knowledge but also to establish it with certainty. It is an odd fact that, in spite of wild variations as to methodology and conclusions, the tradition of modern philosophy has tacitly accepted the task defined by Descartes as a legitimate one.[16]

According to Thorson the path from the program of Descartes to modern philosophy had as its key landmark the philosophical critique of Immanuel Kant, whose concern was to establish that our knowledge can be objective knowledge of a real external world.[17] He proposed that although our minds do impose a rational form on knowledge, the content of that knowledge derives from our experience of an external, objective reality and is therefore not just the invention of our minds. Kant therefore accepted the Cartesian requirement for rational certainty, and then tried to achieve objectivity by restricting the contribution of our personal involvement in knowledge to a logical, rational form. The result was that objectivity became identified with impersonality; the surest way to arrive at objective truth was to avoid personal involvement. The price that was paid for this kind of objectivity was heavy: scientific knowledge was stripped of its human, personal component.

As Thorson expresses it,

There is a price for this sort of "objectivity": if what is objective is necessarily impersonal, then by its very nature what is personal cannot truly be objective. That other half of the Cartesian polarity, the existential ego, to whose "reality" we are all committed de facto—that other half cannot be ignored; so we have the emergence of existentialist philosophy as a fundamentally schizophrenic reaction to the positivist ideals. What began as a polarization in Descartes between the self as knower and the object of his knowledge, eventually became a radical dualism in thought. Tragically, "objectivity" went with one pole, but "meaning" with the other, and modern man has not found it possible to reunite them. Within the Cartesian program, it is impossible.[18]

Faith Revived: All Truth Involves Personal Commitment

A breakthrough in our modern understanding of the nature of truth occurred with the 1966 publication of what Michael Polanyi called his "philosophy of personal knowledge."[19] Polanyi was a physical chemist who, in his later years, turned his mind to the question of how we arrive at truth. He noted that modern thought had created a dualism between fact and meaning, between truth and value, which he felt held dire consequences for the future of our civilization. There had been the beginnings of change in the attitude toward modern philosophy with the insistence of Albert Einstein that all knowledge at whatever level involves an insepara- ble intertwining of theoretical and empirical elements. Einstein argued that though knowledge starts and ends with experience, there is no logical path to that knowledge through deduction from observations, because there is no logical bridge between our ideas and our experience. As Thomas Torrance explains in his *Belief in Science and in Christian Life,* what Einstein proposed was that we employ an intuitive mode of apprehension, resting on a sympa- thetic understanding of nature, to penetrate the intelligible fea- tures inherent in nature.[20] Einstein restored a way of thinking that is not tied exclusively to visible connections but that penetrates behind appearances to an unseen relatedness inherent in nature, which determines appearances. In Einstein's words, "God does not wear his heart on his sleeve."[21] Einstein held a powerful convic- tion of the intelligibility of nature; this controlling belief was at the core of his religious experience.[22]

Einstein's conclusions were born out of his appreciation of the basic change in the structure of physical science ushered in espe- cially by the work of another deeply religious scientist, James Clerk Maxwell. Torrance, in his edited volume *A Dynamical Theory of the Electromagnetic Field,* says of Maxwell's contribution that it was so revolutionary in concept and so completely counter to the ob- session of other scientists for mechanical models that it took some time for his unitary theory of electricity, light, and magnetism to be accepted.[23] Even his close friend Sir William Thomson (Lord Kelvin) stated that in departing from mechanical models Maxwell had lapsed into mysticism. Torrance gives us a character sketch of Maxwell that demonstrates how essential faith was to the freedom with which he hypothesized and formulated:

From his earliest days at Edinburgh Academy and Edinburgh University, Clerk Maxwell had been fascinated with the relation of geometrical forms to motion, and developed new modes of thought, which he put very successfully into effect in several areas of scientific research and theory, in his explanation of the stability of Saturn's rings, in his dynamical theory of gases, in his work in colour vision and colour photography, and above all in his theoretical clarification of our understanding of electricity and magnetism and light through combining them in one electromagnetic theory. From his earliest studies, however, Clerk Maxwell also came to realise the limited applicability of merely analytical mathematics to account for the dynamic modes of connection found in nature, so that even though he himself went further than any other between Newton and Einstein in the rigorous application of mathematical equations to natural phenomena and their behaviour, he was persistently aware of "the vastness of nature and narrowness of our symbolical sciences." No human science, he felt, could ever really match up in its theoretical connections to the real modes of connection existing in nature, for valid as they may be in mathematical and symbolic systems, they were true only up to a point and could only be accepted by men of science, as well as by men of faith, in so far as they were allowed to point human scientific inquiry beyond its own limits to that hidden region where thought weds fact, and where the mental operation of the mathematician and the physical action of nature are seen in their true relation. That is to say, as Clerk Maxwell himself understood it, physical science cannot be rightly pursued without taking into account an all-important metaphysical reference to the ultimate ground of nature's origin in the Creator. Thus while Clerk Maxwell never intruded his theological and deeply evangelical convictions into his physical and theoretical science, he clearly allowed his Christian belief in God the Creator and Sustainer of the universe to exercise some regulative control in his judgment as to the appropriateness and tenability of his scientific theories, that is, as to whether they measured up as far as possible to "the riches of creation." It was in that spirit that he put forward his own theories, always with reserve and always with the demand that they must be put to the test of fact, for his Christian faith would not allow him to fence off any area from critical clarification or to make any other claim for his theories than that they were of a provisional and revisable nature.[24]

These two great scientists, then, were part of the foundation upon which Michael Polanyi built his philosophy of personal knowledge. What Polanyi noted as a common feature of all theorizing in science was that belief in, and commitment to, scientific theories as potentially true, has always been a critical aspect of scientific discovery. What often appeals to us most forcefully is the sense of rational holism that a good theory conveys. But the essential feature is not the power of the rational mind to deal with the abstract, but rather the fact that there are persons who take seriously that theory's capacity to describe the way the world is. It is in the actions of these scientists within the framework of personal commitment that the fruit of science is born. The powerful conclusion we are driven to by Polanyi's extensive analysis is that even in science there is no such thing as abstract knowledge. It is knowledge only when it is held by someone and acted upon as part of a larger whole.

The most telling feature of the idea of personal knowledge is revealed by Polanyi's analysis of what he calls tacit knowledge. He notes that underneath the judgmental and perceptual skills that are applied by the scientist are a set of inarticulate skills and arts that are essential to our theorizing. Criteria such as symmetry, simplicity, elegance, fruitfulness, and satisfaction are not susceptible to logical scrutiny, but they form a significant component of our theorizing. These tacit components may be viewed in the aggregate as different aspects of what the scientist often terms beauty, the sense of which we are often unaware as we seek to build a theoretical framework for our observations. In Thorson's words,

Our sense, and the collective tradition, of beauty—and hence the character of our tacit criteria—is capable of change and development; but unmistakably it is a sense of beauty which moves us to prefer some theories to others, and even to heuristically commit ourselves to them, even though as yet we have no clear conception of their consequences. Now it is a surprising thing that this general expectation regarding reality is not disappointed far more often than it is rewarded, but on the contrary it seems to have a real power to evoke creative vision within the human mind.[25]

Polanyi pointed out that the concept of personal knowledge does not represent a leap into existentialism, but instead involves a radical reappraisal of the concept of objectivity. To appreciate his argument we must go back to the fundamental Judeo-Christian understanding of faith in its relationship to sight and reason. This understanding is that the object of faith substantiates and extends our faith. If in medieval times that understanding was perverted to signify some special forms of insight, some wisdom divinely infused apart from evidential grounds of knowledge, we must recognize it for the error that it was. In the words of Thomas Torrance,

Faith "sees" not with any special faculty of vision on the part of the observer, but with the powers of the reality seen. That is another way of saying that faith is correlated with the intrinsic rationality of the object and its self-evidencing reality and revealing power, which applies in different measure to the functioning of perception and the functioning of faith.[26]

Belief, then, is objectively grounded. The believer has as the object either another person or some other reality independent of himself or herself. People behave rationally when they interact with the other and do not confuse it with themselves. This is, Polanyi says, the way all meaning arises, when we look away from ourselves to something else. His illustration is the use of a stick to explore a cave or the use of a cane by a blind man. The holder is only vaguely aware of the stick in his hand, because all his concentration is focused on the objects contacted through the stick. This from/to relation is also illustrated by the reading of a book. Torrance says,

In reading a book we do not focus our attention on the letters and sentences themselves merely as marks on paper, nor do we treat them as some way of giving expression to ourselves, but we attend to that to which they refer beyond, for it is in that objective reference that their significance lies.[27]

Polanyi's astounding conclusion is, "Truth is something that can be thought of only by believing it."[28]

But what of the object of our belief? According to Polanyi, belief is a cognitive assent to some aspect of reality, a response to a pattern imprinted in the world around us. And this is not just any jumble of observations; it must be a coherent pattern or an orderly structure to which we react with acknowledgment and assent.[29] This kind of objectivity brings to the process of scientific truth-gathering a liberating open-mindedness, because belief arises in our minds through the force of reality and its intrinsic intelligibility. That is, ours is a journey of discovery, a looking forward to new truth, which now is only partially grasped. That is why we can refer to it as faith, for it is directed to a larger reality yet unseen. As Torrance says, "Belief, as Polanyi understands it, . . . is tied up with the fact that we know more than we can tell, that our basic affirmations indicate more than we can specify."[30]

Scientific belief, in this view, also has an element of exclusiveness. For if we believe one thing, that immediately excludes a range of other things. When some theoretical structure receives sufficient support to be defined in terms of a natural law, it achieves a high degree of exclusiveness, which approaches universal acknowledgment. Yet it is still less than absolute as an aspect of truth, for it refers to a reality, as Polanyi says, beyond that which we can completely specify. Indeed, the implication of much of what we have said is that the reality beyond is staggeringly large.

And finally, scientific belief as so described is not unlike theological knowing in the Christian sense. The grace of God comes to us in Jesus Christ unconditionally, but carries with it unconditional obligations, so that faith that is founded on grace involves elements of both freedom and compulsion. What Polanyi says of scientific belief is equally true theologically: "Every belief is both a free gift and a payment of tribute exacted from us."[31]

The salient features of both kinds of knowing are the essential participation of persons and the commitment to an external reality that is required of them.

PROSPECTS FOR A NEW SYNCRETISM BETWEEN THEOLOGY AND SCIENCE

Beyond this, you could reasonably speculate that science approached in this attitude of open expectancy might not only enhance the rate and quality of scientific discovery, but could also be catalytic in its effect on other approaches to knowledge. Ralph Wendell Burhoe, in his edited volume *Science and Human Values in the 21st Century,* sees a tremendous future for such an informed theology:

Let us look at some of the potentials for a theology informed positively by the sciences. . . . there is beginning to arise in the twentieth century a group of scientists who are seers of the unseen hand that rules human destiny. These men have not been very much heard, seen, or understood by the general public or by the religious communities. . . . Gradually, the growing wisdom of the scientific seers or prophets will probably get through to leaders of the Christian community as significant confirmations and extensions of their historic faith. For in reality these scientists are declarers of what the transcendent reality will permit and what it will reject, and hence what is good or bad for each and every living being or system, and what man must do to be saved for fulfillment in higher levels of order or organization of life. I prophesy that from this source man is most likely to find an enlarged vision of purpose and hope, for the credible myth of human meaning in the scheme of things.

What I am trying to suggest here is that the art of religion, like the technology or art of medicine, will be best informed and most able to function adequately in an age of radically new science and technology when that religion is itself informed by currently credible knowledge provided by the sciences.[32]

This syncretism has been the heart's desire of a growing group of scientists, some of whom have reached the pinnacle of success in their chosen field. Rustum Roy, in his book *Experimenting with Truth,* mentions a number of those who have arrived at "a position affirming the Beyond in the midst of equations, galaxies, or conducting electrons, or new organic synthesis of DNA helices."[33] Among these are Alfred North Whitehead, mathematician and philosopher; Sir James Jeans, the British astronomer; Michael Polanyi, Hungarian physical chemist turned philosopher; James Conant, chemist and president of Harvard; Charles Coulson, mathematician and chemist at Oxford; Charles Townes, physics Nobelist; Sir Alistair Hardy, marine biologist and Templeton prize recipient; and Carl Friedrich von Weizacker, physicist and younger associate of Werner Heisenberg. Heisenberg himself provides a probing autobiography of his search for the Beyond in a book entitled *Physics and Beyond.* [34] But Heisenberg brings another important dimension of faith into his science as the essential basis of ethics and values.

Heisenberg was the discoverer of the uncertainty principle, the momentous discovery that excluded the possibility that both position and momentum of elementary particles could simultaneously be known. His discovery, for which he received the Nobel prize in 1932, meant the end of classical physics and rigid determinism, and propelled the physical sciences into the quantum world. It is not surprising, then, that Heisenberg was interested in those aspects of reality that go beyond science, just as the quantum world presented vast philosophical changes for the practitioners of classical physics. In fact, *Physics and Beyond* proves him to be a profound thinker and a deeply sensitive human being. The story of his growth, his choice of physics, his education in prewar Germany at Munich and Göttingen, his close relationships with Niels Bohr, the inventor of quantum theory, and with Wolfgang Pauli, Carl Friedrich von Weizacker, and Hans Euler, and the difficult war years inside Germany, are all fascinating. But his religious views are still more arresting.

Once, in a conversation with Wolfgang Pauli and Paul Dirac, the question of Einstein's talk about God came up, with the expression of considerable surprise that he would have strong ties to a religious tradition. Someone commented that Max Planck was even more religious. Heisenberg then elaborated on Planck's views with sympathy but with an important reservation. He said,

Planck considers science and religion compatible because, in his view, they refer to quite distinct facets of reality. Science deals with the objective, material world. It invites us to make accurate statements about objective reality and to grasp its interconnections. Religion, on the other hand, deals with the world of values. It considers what ought to be or what we ought to do, not what is. . . . In short, the conflict between the two, which has been raging since the eighteenth century, seems founded on a misunderstanding, or more precisely, on a confusion of the images and parables of religion with scientific statements. This view, which I know so well from my parents, associates the two realms with the objective and subjective aspects of the world respectively. But I must confess that I myself do not feel altogether happy about this separation. I doubt whether human societies can live with so sharp a distinction between knowledge and faith.[35]

At a later point in his book, Heisenberg states his belief that the issue of values implies a "compass by which we must steer our ship through life." This compass, he says, is the "central order," the "one" with which we communicate in the language of religion. This religion, he feels, must win out, for the very idea of truth is involved with the reality of religious experiences.[36]

And so we have come back to the theme of right and wrong, of human values as an essential, integral element in our knowing, whether in a scientific or in a theological frame of reference. And what seems increasingly evident is the interconnection of faith and truth as a universal principle, embracing the whole realm of human experience in all times and places, pointing us to the One who constitutes the physical universe and also pervades our very being. As St. Paul said to the Athenians long ago, of "the unknown God," "He is not far from each of us, for in him we live and move and have our being."[37]

NOTES

1. C. S. Lewis, *Mere Christianity* (New York: Macmillan, 1960), 21.
2. Ibid., 30.
3. John Polkinghorne, *The Way the World Is* (Grand Rapids: Eerdmans, 1983), 27, 28.
4. Peter L. Berger, *A Rumor of Angels* (Garden City, N.J.: Anchor Books, 1970).
5. Ibid., 56, 57.
6. Edward E. Evans-Pritchard, *Nuer Religion* (Oxford: Clarendon Press, 1956).
7. William James, *The Varieties of Religious Experience* (New York: Longmans, 1902).
8. Alistair Hardy, *The Living Stream* (London: Collins, 1965).
9. Ibid., 269.
10. Alistair Hardy, *The Spiritual Nature of Man* (Oxford: Oxford University Press, 1979).
11. Hardy, *The Living Stream,* 283.
12. Ibid., 284.

13. Walter R. Thorson, "Spiritual Dimensions of Science," in *Horizons of Science,* ed. C. F. H. Henry (New York: Harper & Row, 1978).

14. R. Hooykaas, *Religion and the Rise of Modern Science* (Edinburgh: Scottish Acad. Press., 1973).

15. Thorson, "Spiritual Dimensions of Science," 241, 242.

16. Walter R. Thorson, "Science as the Natural Philosophy of the Christian," *Journal of American Scientific Affiliation* 33 (1981): 68.

17. Ibid., 70.

18. Ibid., 70.

19. Michael Polanyi, *Personal Knowledge: An Introduction to Post-Critical Philosophy* (New York: Harper Torchbooks, Harper & Row, 1966).

20. Thomas F. Torrance, "The Framework of Belief," Chapter I in *Belief in Science and in Christian Life,* ed. Thomas F. Torrance (Edinburgh: Handsel Press, 1980), 9.

21. F. S. C. Northrop, *Man, Nature and God* (1962), 209.

22. Albert Einstein, *Out of My Later Years* (Secaucus, N.J.: Citadel Press, 1950), 30, 60.

23. Thomas F. Torrance, *A Dynamical Theory of the Electromagnetic Field* (Edinburgh: Scottish Academic Press, 1982), ix–x.

24. Ibid., ix–x.

25. Walter Thorson, "The Biblical Insights of Michael Polanyi," *Journal of American Scientific Affiliation* 33 (1981): 135.

26. Thomas F. Torrance, *Belief in Science and in Christian Life* (Edinburgh: Handsel Press, 1980), 10.

27. Ibid., 11.

28. Polanyi, *Personal Knowledge,* 305.

29. Ibid., 33–48.

30. Torrance, *Belief in Science,* 15.

31. Ibid., 16.

32. Ralph W. Burhoe, ed., *Science and Human Values in the 21st Century* (Philadelphia: Westminster, 1971), 166–67.

33. Rustum Roy, *Experimenting with Truth,* (New York: Pergamon, 1981), 154–55.

34. Werner Heisenberg, *Physics and Beyond* (New York: Harper & Row, 1971).

35. Ibid., 82–83.

36. Ibid., 214–15.

37. Acts 17:27, 28, RSV.

8. The Remarkable Evolution of Humankind

A DIVINE PLAN FOR HUMANKIND

The size of God may be impressed upon us by looking at humankind, at our creativity as expressed in our art and our institutions, at the results of our curiosity and capacity for systemization as measured by our science, but particularly as we realize the immense evolutionary journey that has brought us to this point in our perhaps million-year history.

Throughout, the vast process seems to have been a struggle to define ourselves, and for a significant span of our evolution the scientific data suggests that we have wanted a spiritual relationship to be part of that definition. Indeed, the psalmist places us in an intimate and even timeless relationship with our Creator, and suggests that the spiritual affinity was mutual, and that, in fact, his interest in us began long before we were born into this world. The psalmist David writes,

> For you created my inmost being:
> you knit me together in my mother's womb.
> I praise you because I am
> fearfully and wonderfully
> made:
> your works are wonderful,
> I know that full well.
> My frame was not hidden from you
> when I was made in the
> secret place.
> When I was woven together
> in the depths of the earth
> your eyes saw my

> unformed body.
> All the days ordained for me
> were written in your book
> before one of them came
> to be.[1]

The unique relationship of humankind with the Creator and the creation has been a puzzle and a paradox that philosopher and scientist, poet and theologian have remarked upon. Within the scientific community, neurophysiologist and Nobel laureate Sir John Eccles speaks of the uniquely human "moral point of view," noting the emphasis that this receives in the writings of Socrates.[2] From Eccles's viewpoint it is the culmination of a process that begins with "man's awareness of the fact of his own transcendence; the recognition that human persons are different from and rise above those utterly material events comprised in the purely physical cosmos." It would seem that humankind has always had an ambivalence about the world and its part in it. We have been both practical analyst and mystic. Our present age of scientific understanding and technological sophistication has brought the suggestion that there will soon be no mystery to confound us, that illusion will be a thing of the past and that we will be well rid of it. But in the end we are more beset by the unexplained, with multiplied mysteries to explain, and the ultimate questions remain unanswered. In the words of renowned anthropologist Loren Eiseley,

Man has always had two ways of looking at nature, and these two divergent approaches to the world can be observed among modern primitive peoples, as well as being traceable far into the primitive past. Man has a belief in seen and unseen nature. He is both pragmatist and mystic. He has been so from the beginning, and it may well be that the quality of his inquiring and perceptive intellect will cause him to remain so till the end.

Primitive man, grossly superstitious though he may be, is also scientist and technologist. He makes tools based upon his empirical observation of the simple forces around him. Man would have vanished long ago if he had been content to exist in the wilderness of his own dreams. Instead he compromised. He accepted a world of reality, a natural, everyday, observable world in which he existed, and whose forces he utilized in order to survive. The other aspect of his mind, the mystical part seeking answers to final questions, clothed this visible world in a shimmering haze of magic. Unseen spirits moved in the wood. Today in our sophistication we smile, but we are not satisfied with the appearances of the phenomenal world around us. We wish to pierce beneath to ask the question, "Why does the universe exist?" We have learned a great deal about secondary causes, about the *how* of things. The why, however, eludes us, and as long as this is the case, we will have a yearning for the marvelous, the explosive event in history.[3]

Perhaps the greatest explosion in history is the remarkable rapidity of humankind's own evolution. From the standpoint of time alone, this appearance of Homo sapiens is but a mere tick of the geological clock, perhaps only 200,000 years, but in that brief interval—and particularly during the past 30,000 years—a set of characteristics and capabilities has emerged that profoundly distinguishes humankind from any predecessor. It is as Eiseley says in another context, "Nature's last great play—the play of man."[4]

It is a powerful play, with a challenging role for its central character! It represents the consummation of three billion years of life on Earth; the arrival of a creature who walks erect and has a brain so revolutionary that it gives its possessor the powers of speech, abstract thought, and self-conscious awareness. And with these remarkable endowments, humankind has found the capacity to modify its environment. As Eiseley says,

With the emergence of the human brain, man had, to a previously inconceivable degree, passed out of the domain of the particulate evolution of biological organs and had entered upon what we may call history. Human beings, in whom the power of communication had arisen, were leaving the realm of phylogeny for the realm of history, which was to contain, henceforth, our final destiny.[5]

RECENT SCIENTIFIC FINDINGS CONCERNING HUMAN EVOLUTION

THE COMPRESSED TIME FRAME

Eiseley tells us in *The Immense Journey* that when the warfare that raged around Charles Darwin's theory of life's origins had subsided in the 1870s, there remained for him one disturbing adversary, Alfred Russel Wallace. Wallace, codiscoverer with Darwin of the theory of natural selection, had asked one question: "How did man get his brain?"[6] The answer, for Wallace, was a theological one: the entire evolutionary process was an unfolding of the divine will. His answer was met with considerable objection by Darwin, who, however, supplied no scientifically viable alternative. And in the aftermath of Huxley's persuasive arguments for humankind's anatomical similarity to the apes, Wallace's question was ignored. The basis for Wallace's concern was rooted in the surprisingly rapid development of the human brain, which was so much larger than any of the other primates, and in his knowledge of the intelligence of the natives of the South Seas and the East Indies. In the latter case, he asked why natives, in such primitive surroundings, should be endowed with such excellent brains when their mental powers were greatly in excess of what was needed to carry on simple food-gathering. Wallace's question, Eiseley tells us, was,

How, then, was an organ developed so far beyond the needs of its possessor? Natural selection could only have endowed the savage with a brain a little superior to that of an ape, whereas he actually possesses one but little inferior to that of the average member of our learned societies.[7]

Indeed, the most convincing of the natives' attributes was their language capacity, for Wallace noted that their "capacity of uttering a variety of distinct articulate sounds and of applying to them an almost infinite amount of modulation . . . is not in any way inferior to that of the higher races."[8]

Not only is the human being qualitatively and quantitatively similar in all races and unique in comparison with any other living species of animal, but the probable human precursors seem unique as well. As we move backward in time for the brief evolutionary period of perhaps 300,000 years, the characteristic brain persisted first in Homo sapiens (Neandertal) and then in Homo sapiens (archaic). Both also controlled fire and made tools. Both walked erect, though this characteristic survives in some form all the way back to the Australopithecines, primitive but smaller-brained hominids who are the presumed ancestors of genus Homo. These ancestors lived about two million years ago.[9]

Many anthropologists argue for the uniqueness of bipedality in human evolution, and its essentiality for the eventual increase in brain size, but here again there is the expression of surprise at the rapid onset of bipedality, which is anatomically impossible in any presently known apes or monkeys. Early Australopithecines, such as the now-famous Lucy, who lived three million years ago, had unique bone and muscle structure, with a flared pelvis and high muscles attached at the sides of the thigh, in contrast to the ape's long pelvis with muscles attached at the back. These differences, together with leg bones that turned inward to make Lucy walk a bit knock-kneed, enabled her to walk erect instead of emulating the rocking, stooped posture of a primate such as a chimpanzee.[10]

We are left with the question that Wallace asked Darwin, and we can now add the question, How did human bipedality evolve? Both the complex brain and bipedality appear to have arisen in a very brief interval of evolutionary history.

The Remarkable Human Brain

Comparative Anatomy and Physiology of the Brain

The evolutionary process is often described in its broadest terms as a 15-billion-year process, which begins with the big bang, proceeds through the evolution of stars and galaxies, and ends with the appearance of life—and in the last few moments with the appearance of conscious life. If we attribute to the human brain the unique capacity for conscious thought, then that event has been with us, at least on this planet, for only one thirty-thousandth of the history of the cosmos. Yet from the standpoint of its complexity and its capability, the human brain was surely worth the wait. Concerning complexity, in its three pounds the human brain packs 10 billion nerve cells and nearly 100 billion supporting cells. Recall from Chapter 3 that the number of connections from each nerve cell to its neighbors averages upward of five thousand. The aggregate complexity of this connectedness is of the same order as the number of stars in the universe. Furthermore, unlike a computer, where individual units are switches that are either on or off, in the brain the nerve cell units are themselves highly complicated structures, each with a repertoire of responses to stimuli. The human brain is by far the most complicated organization of matter in the universe![11]

Here, too, a remarkable evolution of structure and function has occurred, beginning with the simple brain of reptiles, proceeding upward in complexity through the mammals, primates, and early hominids, to the highly sophisticated organ of the modern human. The human brain is divided into the hindbrain, midbrain, and forebrain. The hindbrain includes the cerebellum, in the back of the skull, which coordinates movement, and the lower brain stem, which functions as the gate through which sensory and motor signals travel from the spinal cord to the rest of the brain. The midbrain is the upper portion of the brain stem, and carries out the relay of certain sensory stimuli. The forebrain contains the cerebral hemispheres and the cortex, limbic system, and diencephalon. The most primitive parts of the brain appear to be the cerebellum and brain stem. The next oldest feature is the diencephalon, which contains the thalamus, another gate for sensory stimuli, and the hypothalamus, which performs a variety of regulatory functions, including the control of blood pressure, body temperature, and appetite. Also present in the diencephalon are the pituitary, with functions in growth control, and the pineal gland, an internal clock regulating sleep and other light-sensitive cycles.

Outward from the diencephalon is the next most recent evolutionary addition to the brain, the limbic system, which houses the olfactory bulb, the smell-sensing organ, and several components that combine to control the emotions. Among these components are the S-shaped hippocampus and the amygdala, both of which are also involved in memory functions.

Finally we come to a recent addition to the brain, the cerebrum, which wraps around the rest of the brain and makes up, in the human, two-thirds of the brain's weight. It is composed of two hemispheres, each of which has four lobes: occipital, temporal, parietal, and frontal. Each lobe in the left hemisphere has its counterpart in the right hemisphere, but the two sides generally have different functions. Oddly enough, cerebral function has a mirror-like quality. The left hemisphere controls the right side of the body, and the right hemisphere the left side. So, too, the visual fields are reversed, with the left visual field sending signals to the brain's right half, and the right visual field transmitting to the left half. Enclosing the entire eight-lobed structure of the cerebrum is the neocortex, the most recent evolutionary addition to the brain, a thin sheet of tissue that is highly folded and convoluted and includes more than half of the brain's neurons. It is this structure that is the most enlarged and elaborated in the human brain.

The four types of lobes of the cerebrum have different functions. The occipital lobes, at the rear, are concerned with visual processing. The temporal lobes interact with the limbic system, and so are concerned with emotional activities as well as significant processing of auditory stimuli. The parietal lobes arch across the top of the brain, and contain the motor and sensory cortex, two independent structures that behave like topographic maps with individual segments of neurons delegated to respond to each sensory or motor area in the body. Finally, the frontal lobes, just behind the forehead, are involved, in a less well defined way, with what might be called self-awareness and also the sense of relationship to others. It is this area that has undergone the greatest evolutionary change. Judith Hooper and Dick Teresi, in their book *The 3-Pound Universe,* describe the evolutionary aspect as follows:

What the frontal lobes "control" is something like awareness, or self-awareness, which is hard to quantify. Consider: The frontal cortex of rats is minute. In cats it occupies a paltry 3.5 percent of the cortex. In chimpanzees the figure has risen to 17 percent. But in Homo sapiens it's a whopping 29 percent. The ratio of frontal cortex to the rest of the cortex may be one index of evolutionary advancement. Do these lobes govern some essential feature of humanness, or even godliness, as some scientists have suggested? "If God speaks to man, if man speaks to God," neuroscientist Candace Pert tells us, "it would be through the frontal lobes, which is the part of the brain that has undergone the most recent evolutionary expansion."

Paul MacLean, for one, considers the frontal lobes the "heart" of the cortex. He observes, "In the progress from Neanderthal to Cro-Magnon man, one sees the forehead develop from a low brow to a high brow. Underneath that heightened brow is the prefrontal cortex. . . . The prefrontal cortex is the only part of the neocortex that looks inward to the inside world. Clinically, there is evidence that the prefrontal cortex by looking inward, so to speak, obtains the gut feeling required for identifying with another individual." In other words, empathy.[12]

But there's more to the unique human brain than the greatly enlarged frontal cortex, even though it is, in the words of neural scientist Paul MacLean, "the mother of invention and the father of abstract thought."[13] When we look at the limbic system, the emotional center, we first see an apparently primitive survival mechanism that operates by the balance of pain and pleasure. But studies in MacLean's laboratory in which the neocortex of hamsters was severed indicates that the distinctively mammalian functions of play, nursing, and maternal care are functions of the cingulate gyrus, the most recent evolutionary addition to the limbic system. And, too, the limbic system and the temporal cortex have some special relationship that appears to involve another aspect of self-awareness, for in cases of disruption, such as temporal lobe epilepsy, the patient often expresses strong religious feelings, moral indignation when someone is wronged, sudden recollections of past events, and even true deja vu.[14]

Beyond the cerebral cortex and the limbic system, the remainder of the brain, much older from an evolutionary standpoint, appears to be rather inflexible and to operate more on an instinctive rather than a learning basis. This is the kind of brain found in simpler organisms: honey bees, whose communicative dances are stereotyped; frogs, who have instinctive responses to flying insects; goslings, which on first hatching immediately "attach" to the mother goose; and (by contrast) lizards, which bite at the first thing that moves. Humans have a good deal of such "hard-wired" behavior too, stipulated by relatively rigid genetic determinants, but the essential difference lies in the much larger proportion of "soft-wired" gray matter in the human brain.[15]

The Unique Capacity for Language

Perhaps the most astounding attribute of the human brain is its capacity for language; this appears to be an example of the combination of "hard" and "soft" wiring. We noted earlier that Alfred Russel Wallace had observed that even the most primitive cultures used languages of a sophistication comparable to that of modern cultures. Recent linguistic studies not only confirm this notion but say that all languages have common rules that lie beneath the observable surface of spoken sentences. Jeremy Campbell, in his fascinating book *Grammatical Man,* tells us that one of the leaders in this area of research is linguist and information theorist Noam Chomsky, who in the 1950s proposed that sentences are generated through a series of rules that are part of the brain's coded information.[16] These rules may be utilized repeatedly in conjunction with a finite vocabulary to provide an unlimited variety of properly formed sentences. One of the questions that this theory of language answered related to the rapidity with which children learn a language, despite only limited exposure to random samples of adult speech. Innate principles guide the child to the correct rules of sentence formation; in effect, to a correct theory of language.

What appears to be a second consequence of this internal coding for proper use of languages is the fact that all languages show a surprising stability over long periods of use. This appears to explain why even the most ancient languages are highly complex. In Campbell's words,

It is one of the curious facts about languages that they are always rich in structure, no matter what their time and place in the history of known tongues. The languages that "backward" people speak are not primitive.

In fact, there is no such thing as a primitive language. All are highly complex. Nor does language decay and fall into disorder, as one might suppose. Languages tend to preserve intelligibility, so that what may appear to be decay at a present time is not really decay at all. It is the replacement of one kind of structure by another kind.[17]

The suggestion of these studies is that human beings have this remarkable and unique capacity for communication by means of complex verbal expression as a consequence of a unique biological event: the evolution of the human brain. Again, in Campbell's words,

The whole question of complexity is one which has proved surprisingly subtle when investigated by modern theorists. Complexity is not just a matter of a system having a lot of parts which are related to one another in nonsimple ways. Instead, it turns out to be a special property in its own right, and it makes complex systems different in kind from simple ones, enabling them to do things and be things we might not have expected. Chomsky suggests that human language competence, which must be among the most complicated structures in the universe, arises uniquely in evolution at a certain stage of biological complexity. In other words, it appears when, and only when, evolution has led to an organism as complex as a human being.[18]

The Unique Timetable of Human Brain Development

Anthropologist Loren Eiseley, in his book *The Immense Journey*, tells us that the evolution of the brain turned a corner when human beings arrived on the scene a half-million years ago.[19] A major problem had to be faced. Here was a brain more than twice the size of that of the largest primates, which therefore had to develop with great rapidity during infancy. Yet if this growth was confined to the fetal period, as with the apes, the head would be so large at birth that passage through the birth canal, already difficult in humans, would be impossible. Therefore this greatly accelerated growth had to take place subsequent to birth. When we are born our brain size is about 330 cubic centimeters, only slightly larger than that of a baby gorilla. In the first six months after birth, the ape brain has reached virtually full size. But with the human brain, an extraordinary thing happens. The brain goes right on developing, more than doubling in size in the first year, increasing by 25 percent in the second year, and by an additional 15 percent in the third. Furthermore, this development appears to be innovative, not "hard-wired," because the right- and left-sidedness of the brain appears to be established only at age six or seven. Richard Restak, in his book *The Brain,* tells us that a stroke in a young child often has no effect on subsequent language development, whereas the same stroke in an adult is often devastating, leading to severe and often permanent loss of speech function.[20] The difference is probably because the two hemispheres provide backup systems for each other in the event of damage to one. Furthermore, before the advent of modern obstetrics, birth injury to the brain was much more common. Injury that required removal of one hemisphere led to the complete takeover of functions of both hemispheres by the remaining functional half. These and other data suggest a qualitatively different developmental program in the maturing human brain.

This slowing down of maturation, retaining into adulthood the juvenile traits of ancestral species, is called neoteny.[21] This process is found among other creatures, but only in humans does it involve the brain. In the human brain it is all the more remarkable, because the coding sequences of DNA in humans and apes are so similar. Humans and chimpanzees differ by only 1 percent in the gene sequences that code for specific protein products. Yet their structural dissimilarities are many. We have remarked on the differences that lead to the erect walk in human beings compared to the stooped posture of apes. The difference in brain size is tremendous. But how do we explain the lack of differences at the molecular level, as indicated by the similar DNA sequences? The explanation may well lie in the way the genetic information is read, especially in the timing of its readout. Campbell proposes that neoteny may be such a program, undetectable by DNA homology studies because it is a kind of algorithm, in the same way that the universal grammar, the built-in brain information for language proficiency, is an algorithm.[22] The consequences of this new program for brain development are manifold. To quote Campbell,

Timing the expression of genes in the growing organism has turned out to be a process which is much more than a marvelously intricate illustration of how nature uses information to organize matter. We are talking here about something a great deal more remarkable: the hypothesis that a change in the timing of gene expression thrust *Homo sapiens* onto the stage of prehistory and made possible the massive, slow-maturing brain of a species which can do more than merely perceive its world and act immediately upon what it perceives. The human brain provides a significant space between perception and action: in this space arose complex forms of abstract knowledge and the fruits of the contemplative mind: myth, religion, art, literature, and philosophy.[23]

This "significant space," this interval of time in the developing child for experiencing and learning, means that genus Homo is much less bound by automatic or instinctive traits in its genetic endowment. The shift is then possible to a dependency on the social framework and close personal relationships afforded by the family, with a whole new set of interactions that allows for both individual and interactive learning.

AWESOME EVENTS IN THE ICE AGE

The historical context in which this extraordinary transformation of the brain occurred is equally remarkable. The first hint of the use of tools by hominids had been dated at about 500,000 years ago. This was based upon an estimate of one million years ago for the onset of the Ice Age. But Loren Eiseley tells us that the dating of the Ice Age, with the advances and recessions of the ice sheet across Europe and Asia, has undergone considerable revision in the past few decades.[24] Sophisticated dating techniques utilizing the isotope oxygen-18 have been applied to the lime deposits in ancient marine cores, and have demonstrated that the beginning of the first glaciation of Europe was probably no earlier than 500,000 years ago. This finding compresses the evolution of humankind into a scant 350,000 years. This is an astoundingly brief period for the remarkable evolution of humankind. Eiseley comments,

What are we to think of the story of man? Into what foreshortened and cramped circumstances is the human drama to be reduced, a drama, moreover, which, besides evolutionary change, involves time for the spread of man into the New World? Such an episode, it is obvious, would involve a complete reexamination of our thinking upon the subject of human evolution.[25]

The geography of this emergence of human beings is now beginning to be understood. The immediate precursor of the first human was Homo erectus, whose origin is believed to be in Africa. Erectus appears to have already attained a brain size nearly three-quarters of that of sapiens, and to have mastered the art of making stone tools and of controlling fire. This more complicated brain provided the capability for mobility and adaptability, and Homo erectus appears to have migrated across all of Africa and into much of Asia. The characteristic tools of Homo erectus are found in Europe, though oddly, no skeletal remains have been found there.

It is at this point that the great leap occurs to truly human creatures, Homo neandertal. Several writers point out that the Neandertals, the cave dwellers of the cartoonists, have been shamefully maligned; in fact, they are often still depicted as primitive and brutish, with an apelike, knuckle-dragging walk. Eiseley explains,

By Darwinian standards, these creatures were an odd and unimagined link with the past. Their skulls, in spite of jutting brow ridges and massive chinless faces, had brains as large as or larger than our own. Huxley, the swashbuckling evolutionist, hesitated over their meaning with the reluctance of a choirboy. Darwin saw them as armed with gorilloid fangs, and an artist pictured them with the grasping feet of apes. A distinguished anatomist spoke of them as "the quintessence of brute-benightedness."[26]

The true picture of the Neandertals, which is now developing, is one of an intelligent, compassionate, and artful people, who were more robust and stocky than later humans. As Kenneth Weaver tells us, their brains, which were as large if not larger than ours, were housed in large skulls with heavy brow ridges that tended to curve over the eye sockets. Cheekbones were receding, chins were weak, and they had large, protruding jaws. Neandertals had to face a severe climate, and they took refuge in caves and rock shelters. Their tools were rather sophisticated, finely shaped, and oriented toward dressing hides and fashioning clothing. They chewed animal hides to soften them, just as do present-day Eskimos.[27]

One additional anatomical feature characteristic of the modern human appears to have been present in the Neandertals, according to Richard Restak. The skulls of these early people exhibit an internal groove that is related to a brain feature called the Sylvian fissure, a deep cleft in the outer surface of the brain in the vicinity of the speech centers. The significance of the cleft in humans is that it is longer and more horizontally placed in the left hemisphere, an indication of the characteristic asymmetry of the complex human brain. The Neandertal brain exhibits the same asymmetry, and suggests that their brain was not only comparable to ours in size but also in complexity.[28]

Further evidence for the high degree of development of the brain in Neandertals regards their burial practices. As Weaver explains, they were the first to bury their dead, and they apparently did so with solemnity and clearly with some expectation of an afterlife. They included flowers in the burial,[29] and they provided for the departed such things as tools and food, in the way the Egyptians provisioned their tombs.[30] Eiseley gives a description of what was found in a little French cave near La Chapelle-aux-Saints in 1908:

Massive flint-hardened hands had shaped a sepulcher and placed flat stones to guard the dead man's head. A haunch of meat had been left to aid the dead man's journey. Worked flints, a little treasure of the human dawn, had been poured lovingly into the grave. And down the untold centuries the message had come without words: "We too were human, we too suffered, we too believed that the grave is not the end. We too, whose faces affright you now knew human agony and human love."

It is important to consider that across fifty thousand years nothing has changed or altered in that act. It is the human gesture by which we know a man, though he looks out upon us under a brow reminiscent of the ape.[31]

Compassion was directed not only to the dead and bereaved, but also to the living. Social bonds were already strong, as evidenced by some skeletons that displayed broken bones that had healed, and by some that suggested severe arthritis of the hip, diseased vertebrae, and severe tooth loss. Clearly the sick and the crippled were not discarded by the Neandertals![32]

Neandertals apparently used a variety of symbol systems, because zigzag images and parallel lines have been found engraved on bones excavated at their campsites; the same kind of symbol usage flourished in the succeeding culture of the Cro-Magnons. This observation further establishes the high capacity of the human brain for intellectual activity even in the first civilizations. Campbell quotes the British archaeologist Clive Gamble:

It is no longer sufficient to look at human evolution over the past 300,000 years as simply a process of increasing intelligence and offer an explanation in terms of changes in the brain . . . recent studies have demonstrated the existence, some 300,000 years ago, of mental ability equivalent to that of modern man. The dramatic developments in material culture, such as the appearance of art, now seem to be more closely related to changes in the amount and kind of information needed by paleolithic societies, rather than being dependent on the evolution of the brain.[33]

When we come to the later Cro-Magnon or Homo sapiens, we find an explosion of artistic expression and symbolic usage taking place at about the conclusion of the Ice Age, some twenty-five thousand years ago. There is represented in this very ancient phenomenon all of the breadth of human expression we would expect to find in a fine modern art collection. It would seem that some of the cave paintings were drawn for the sheer pleasure of the artist. G. K. Chesterton describes one such encounter with this art in his book *The Everlasting Man:*

They were drawings or paintings of animals; and they were drawn or painted not only by a man but by an artist. Under whatever archaic limitations, they showed that love of the long sweeping or the long wavering line which any man who has ever drawn or tried to draw will recognise; and about which no artist will allow himself to be contradicted by any scientist. They showed the experimental and adventurous spirit of the artist, the spirit that does not avoid but attempts difficult things; as where the draughtsman had represented the action of the stag when he swings his head clean round and noses towards his tail, an action familiar enough in the horse. But there are many modern animal painters who would set themselves something of a task in rendering it truly. In this and twenty other details it is clear that the artist had watched animals with a certain interest and presumably a certain pleasure. In that sense it would seem that he was not only an artist but a naturalist.[34]

More than two hundred caves in Europe have revealed cave drawings, all tracing to this upper paleolithic period twenty thousand to thirty thousand years ago. Indeed, there is such a sudden explosion of paintings and small sculptures that scholars have searched for explanations beyond aesthetic pleasure. One view holds that the caves served as temples of a hunting society, and the paintings were designed to invoke success in the hunt.[35] But critics of this view point out that few of the cave drawings depict animals pierced with arrows and spears. Alternatively, it has been suggested that the caves had a ceremonial or religious aspect, perhaps as decorations of a burial site. One other intriguing possibility suggests itself, especially when the large variety of carved figures are examined. Campbell explains that Alexander Marshack of the Peabody Museum at Harvard believes that the early human possessed powers of abstraction far beyond those of a mere toolmaker and hunter. For example, microscopic examination of one set of carved figures found in a cave in southern Germany revealed symbolic markings, some involving "intricate geometrical patterns of multiple curves and sets of straight lines of different lengths."[36]

Another object, an oval plaque of antler or bone, found in a French cave, seems to be a complex device carrying a code for storing information. Campbell notes that the miniature scale of the engraving, requiring great precision, suggests a well-established tradition. Marshack suggests that several such symbol systems were in existence during the transition from Homo neandertal to Homo sapiens.[37]

Furthermore, analysis of the caves themselves suggests that paintings and engravings were organized according to preconceived plans, explains Bruce Bower in an article in *Science News*. Relationships appear to exist "between paint color, type of signs, species of animal and location within the cave."[38] French scholars believe at least some caves may have served as classrooms, where complex symbol systems were passed on from parent to child.

The conclusion of this analysis of human prehistory is that a stunning event occurred, an emergence of startling proportions, far more rapid than is explicable by any gradual process mediated by the pressures of survival. The advent of humanity shouts of purpose and meaning. Looking at the past, at our past, which in sum appears much more noble than benighted, prompts us to wonder what marvelous ingredient, what great plan distinguishes humankind from all that has gone before.

THE FORCE BEHIND HUMAN EVOLUTION

THE SELFISH GENE

Many minds have struggled with the intriguing implications of the evolutionary process, especially as it relates to humankind. We recall Alfred Russel Wallace's conclusion of more than a century ago in favor of a divine direction of human evolution. Admittedly, in the interim, the role of God in the affairs of humankind has been relegated by many to the place of myth. But in the end it seems they have succeeded only in replacing one set of myths with others. We are all incurable believers!

For many the driving force for human evolution is still survival,

though for the neo-Darwinians it is survival less in terms of struggle and more in terms of reproductive success. For Richard Dawkins survival is instead measured in terms of genes.[39] Darwin had
struggled especially with a proper understanding of altruistic behavior, a very human characteristic observed even in the Neandertals. Although such behavior with a group increases the chance of
survival of the group, a paradox presents itself when the focus is
on the individual. For altruistic behavior on the part of an individual reduces that individual's chance of survival (to reproduce),
which should eventually lead to the loss of that characteristic from
the group. In order to protect the principle of individual selection,
biologists, including Dawkins, have proposed that altruistic behavior be represented instead as genetic *selfishness*. What we call
altruistic behavior, on the part of an individual on behalf of the
group, is really only a mechanism his or her genes have devised
to preserve those genes the individual shares with the rest of the
group. By Dawkins's estimate, evolution began as a group of replicating molecules that constructed for themselves survival machines, vehicles for continuing existence. Crude at first, these
survival machines gradually improved under the pressure of competition. Four billion years later, the replicators had also found
human bodies to serve their ends. In Dawkins's words,

Now they swarm in huge colonies, safe inside gigantic lumbering robots,
sealed off from the outside world, communicating with it by tortuous
indirect routes, manipulating it by remote control. They are in you and
me; they created us, body and mind; and their preservation is the ultimate
rationale for our existence. They have come a long way, those replicators.
Now they go by the name of genes, and we are their survival machines.[40]

Sociobiologists have embraced this idea, first elaborated by Edward Wilson in his monumental work *Sociobiology—The New Synthesis,*[41] but it now appears to have been built on a rather shaky
foundation. Recent developments in the study of the biogenesis of
replicating molecules indicate a staggering level of required complexity, which would seem to require far more information in the
earliest genetic systems than would be available without supernatural intervention.[42] Then, too, the critics of sociobiology have

been many, for it is fundamentally a statement of biological determinism, affirming present institutions as the result of genetic selection and thereby denying social progress. As Lewontin et al. argue in *Not in Our Genes,*

What falls in the realm of necessity falls outside the realm of justice. The issue of justice arises only when there is choice . . . to the extent that we are free to make ethical decisions that can be translated into practice, biology is irrelevant; to the extent that we are bound by our biology, ethical judgments are irrelevant.[43]

The ultimate statement of biological determinism is that we are machines, that every thought or movement is dictated by some structure or function that is ultimately a product of our genes. The sagest critics of this philosophy point out that it is fortunate that its proponents are less committed to this thesis at the level of their personal relationships with their spouses, their families, and their close friends and colleagues.

THE STAR THROWER

For some, then, evolution is an amazing and efficient process whereby genes have engineered ways to preserve themselves. Genes, which must "know" what is best in some sense, become the basis for a belief system. But there are others who have looked long and hard at the remarkable evolution of humankind and have seen it, still as natural process, but in strange, mysterious, ever-elusive, and often poignant ways. Loren Eiseley, whose prose opens to us again and again the wonder of our world and its creatures, nevertheless leaves us with a feeling that humankind has somehow lost its way in a process that may or may not have had it in mind. For Eiseley, the underlying theme is change, process, a relentless instability in which form dissolves into new form, "the eternal struggle of the immediate species against its dissolution into something other," as he says in *The Unexpected Universe.* It is not biological determinism that wins, but the opposite. As he puts it, "The dance of contingency, of the indeterminable, outwits us all." For him, form is only an illusion of the dimension of time, which clings desperately to its identity, striving "to contain the creative and abolishing maelstrom that pours unseen through the generations."[44] For Eiseley, meaning in all this is derived from his everywhere-evident fascination with and love for life. Perhaps his best example is the star thrower, the man he meets on the beach in Cristobal, who walks the shore and seeks to save the hapless starfish that have been washed up by the pounding surf. Eiseley describes the encounter:

Ahead of me, over the projecting point, a gigantic rainbow of incredible perfection had sprung shimmering into existence. Somewhere toward its foot I discerned a human figure standing, as it seemed to me, within the rainbow, though unconscious of his position. He was gazing fixedly at something in the sand.

Eventually he stooped and flung the object beyond the breaking surf. I labored toward him over a half mile of uncertain footing. By the time I reached him the rainbow had receded ahead of us, but something of its color still ran hastily in many changing lights across his features. He was starting to kneel again.

In a pool of sand and silt a starfish had thrust its arms up stiffly and was holding its body away from the stifling mud.

"It's still alive," I ventured.

"Yes," he said, and with a quick yet gentle movement he picked up the star and spun it over my head and far out into the sea. It sank in a burst of spume, and the waters roared once more.

"It may live," he said, "if the offshore pull is strong enough." He spoke gently, and across his bronzed worn face the light still came and went in subtly altering colors.

"There are not many come this far," I said, groping in a sudden embarrassment for words. "Do you collect?"

"Only like this," he said softly, gesturing amidst the wreckage of the shore. "And only for the living." He stooped again, oblivious of my curiosity, and skipped another star neatly across the water.

"The stars," he said, "throw well. One can help them."

He looked full at me with a faint question kindling in his eyes, which seemed to take on the far depths of the sea.

"I do not collect," I said uncomfortably, the wind beating at my garments. "Neither the living nor the dead. I gave it up a long time ago. Death is the only successful collector." . . . I nodded and walked away, leaving him there upon the dune with that great rainbow ranging up the sky behind him.

I turned as I neared a bend in the coast and saw him toss another star, skimming it skillfully far out over the ravening and tumultuous water. For a moment, in the changing light, the sower appeared magnified, as though casting larger stars upon some greater sea. He had, at any rate, the posture of a god.[45]

Few have said it this well, but many have expressed their love for life, of all creatures, as their most fulfilling feeling. It is as though an understanding of the vast evolutionary process has given rise to a deep sense of camaraderie, of kinship with all living things, and our attempt to preserve it is in some very real sense a means for our own perpetuation.

THE GRAND DESIGN

Eiseley leaves us not only with this reverence and love for life, but he wonders, as do all human beings, what lies beyond. Is there somewhere a Thrower, who also struggles, even unsure of the end toward which he labors? And is that uncertainty bound up somehow in the freedom he has given us to explore the unknown, to define our own frontier?[46] Another poet, King David, shared a similar feeling about the God that he knew in the psalm with which we began this chapter. It was as if God was not only the great Knower of our every secret, but that he was intimately involved in our vast pilgrimage. Recall the last verse we quoted from Psalm 139: "All the days ordained for me were written in your book before one of them came to be."

The biblical message is fraught with meaning and purpose and intimacy. The source of humankind and indeed of all creation is God. He *speaks* the universe into being: first light, then Earth and heavens, land and seas and life. And at the end, on the sixth day, humankind.[47] The creation of man—male and female—is described with these profound words:

Then God said, "Let us make man in our image, in our likeness, and let them rule over the fish of the sea and the birds of the air, over the livestock, over all the earth, and over all the creatures that move along the ground."

So God created man in his own image, in the image of God he created him: male and female he created them.[48]

And then in the second chapter, we read this about the creation of humankind:

And the Lord God formed man from the dust of the ground and breathed into his nostrils the breath of life and man became a living being.[49]

What could the writer mean by God creating humans "in his own image"? How could humankind emulate God, especially when we find in Chapter 2 that we are merely "dust of the ground"?

Arthur Peacocke suggests, in his *Creation and the World of Science,* that the clue may lie in God's immanence. Our theology has been directed so heavily toward God's transcendence that we have tended to ignore his identification in and with the physical processes of the universe. Part of the problem, Peacocke says, is our preference for attributing to God the "active, powerful, external adjectives popularly associated with masculinity rather than the more passive, responsive, internal adjectives popularly associated with femininity."[50] With a balanced view, he suggests, we may see God creating a world that is other than himself but, at the same time, *within* himself.

But if God would be our Knower, he would also be the Communicator, the Light-giver.

It is not accidental that light is the first created thing in the Genesis account! It is Peacocke's thought that God communicates to his Creation meaning in and through the network of causal physical processes that have led to our world. And the fruition of those processes has led finally to the human brain, with its staggering capability of understanding both itself and the surrounding world. God gives a creature of his world the power of discernment, the ability to explore and to ponder, and, to some extent, to understand his world. The Communicator has built meaning into his world, and then revealed that meaning through humankind and its remarkable evolution. So, in a profound sense, God the Great

Revealer has created us to be revealers as well; we are made in his image. As Peacocke expresses it,

In man, the stuff of the world has become persons. . . . They are self-conscious free agents, that have been generated by natural processes within the natural order, immanent in which is the transcendent Creator. No wonder the ancient writer said that "God created man in his own image, in the image of God created he him: Male and female created he them." For, in man physicality has become capable of reading those meanings in existence which are the immanence of the transcendent God in the whole cosmic process. The way in which God has made himself heard and understood is by endowing the stuff of the world with the ability to acquire discernment of his meanings and to listen to his word in creation. . . . Creation is an expression of the purpose and intention of God and these purposes have expressed themselves in and through a cosmic evolutionary process which has generated within the physical fabric of the cosmos, beings (ourselves) who can *listen* and *discern.* [51]

The rest of the story of human evolution, up to our present level of social and cultural development, is punctuated by the emergence of certain individuals within the species Homo sapiens in whom discernment seems present to a remarkable degree. We suspect that the Creator found a special pleasure in such individuals as Aristotle, Mozart, da Vinci, and Einstein, limited though each was to his own time and culture.

And of course the biblical revelation gives one salient addition to the human figures who have come into our world. The Apostle John, in the Fourth Gospel, introduces us to Jesus Christ as the God-man, the "Word," who was there at the beginning, and suggests again the intimacy of the relationship of God with his creatures: "When all things began, the Word already was. The Word dwelt with God, and what God was, the Word was . . . through him all things came to be. All that came to be was alive with his life, and that life was the light of man." [52]

Most profoundly, it is said by the writer to the Hebrews that this Son of God is unique in being the perfect representation of God, the "express image of his person." [53] Here is the ultimate "image of God" in human form. The figure of Christ is of universal meaning. The Gospel writers offer him as the "Word made flesh," the "Lamb of God," the sacrifice for humankind's sin and estrangement from the Creator God.[54] The French mystic Pierre Teilhard de Chardin sees the Christ as also the great force behind the process of evolution; at one and the same time he is its energy and its consummation, "Christ the evolver."[55]

Whatever God's detailed purposes in human evolution, his is a gigantic cosmic plan with still more to reveal to the inquisitive and creative brain of humankind. God has indeed written large on our universe, so that all could see him and that some might wonder and worship. It is both exalting and humbling to scan the 200,000 years of our journey. We have come a long way, and we sense an enormous potential still unlocked within us. Within the Christian framework, perhaps retired medical missionary Arden Almquist says it best, in his "Ode to a Pet Chimpanzee":

> I miss you, Daisy.
> You were my link to Africa
> and other things primeval.
> What a mix you were of Genesis
>   and Revelation!
> Clasping your hand
> I seemed at once to grasp
>   Beginnings
> and to reach for the Eschaton;
> and to walk with you
> was to cross dreamily the spans
>   between.
> In the glisten of your dark and searching eyes
> the eons slowly furled. . . .
> You took my near-empty glass
> to bottoms-up my drink,
> and together we thirsted the parch
>   of Pliocene.
> You climbed my mosquito net
>   pole, probing the privacy of my
>   bedroom,
> and in the half-light of the early
>   dawn

we scaled together the scarp of
  Olduvai.
Roguishly you sat in my wastebasket—
a perfect fit—
and there we were again,
resting in a cave in Zimbabwe,
contemplating the antelope femur
  in a baboon hand,
thinking thoughts of internecine
  war.
I looked at you, and saw
God play with cosmic rays
and interplanetary hosts descend to
  earth at His command.
He stirred the primate gene pool
like an artist mixing oils and
  choosing;
and suddenly your clan
stood
celebrated
made tools
and laughed.
I loved you then;
I held you in my arms
wondering. . . .
Then I saw a people formed:
Adam and Eve, Abraham and
  Sarai;
Moses, Miriam, and Joshua;
Samuel and David, Ruth and Esther;
Elijah, Daniel, and John.
Again the angels came;
fearfully Mary accepted the
  heavenly chromosomes—
a Virgin still;
and there was Jesus. . . .
It's a long way back from Him to you,
and just a hairy finger's breadth
  from you to me.

> Often I feel
> I am more like you than Him,
> Daisy.
> Maybe that's why I miss you.[56]

Yet the Scriptures tell us that God humbled himself in becoming the God-man, Jesus.[57] Here we conclude that even the flower of humankind, of whom the temple guards of Jesus' day said, "Never man spake like this man,"[58] was still but an image of the God of the universe.

NOTES

1. Ps. 139:13–18, NIV.
2. Sir John Eccles, *The Wonder of Being Human* (Boston: New Science Library, Shambhala Publications, 1985), ix.
3. Loren Eiseley, *The Firmament of Time* (New York: Atheneum, 1984), 3–4.
4. Loren Eiseley, *The Invisible Pyramid* (New York: Charles Scribner and Sons, 1970), 18.
5. Ibid., 19.
6. Loren Eiseley, *The Immense Journey* (New York: Vintage Books, Random House, 1957), 79.
7. Ibid., 83–84.
8. Ibid., 84.
9. Mary D. Leakey, "NOVA: The Children of Eve," WGBH-TV, Boston, Jan. 31, 1987.
10. Kenneth F. Weaver, "The Search for Our Ancestors," *National Geographic* (November 1985), 560–623.
11. Judith Hooper and Dick Teresi, *The 3-Pound Universe* (New York: Macmillan, 1986), 30–45.
12. Ibid., 42–43.
13. Ibid., 43.
14. Ibid., 48. Also observations of one of the authors (RLH) as a member of the psychosurgery committee of Boston City Hospital, in interaction with Drs. Vernon Mark and Paul Bloomer, 1973–76. See also V. H. Mark and F. R. Ervin, *Violence and the Brain* (New York: Harper & Row, 1965).
15. Ibid., 50.
16. Jeremy Campbell, *Grammatical Man* (New York: Simon and Schuster, 1982), 95–96.
17. Ibid., 99.
18. Ibid., 102.
19. Eiseley, *The Immense Journey,* 109.
20. Richard M. Restak, *The Brain* (Toronto: Bantam Books, 1984), 239–40.
21. Campbell, *Grammatical Man,* 139–41.
22. Ibid., 138.

23. Ibid., 141.
24. Eiseley, *The Immense Journey,* 112–16.
25. Ibid., 113.
26. Eiseley, *The Firmament of Time,* 104–5.
27. Weaver, "The Search for Our Ancestors," 614.
28. Restak, *The Brain,* 241.
29. Campbell, *Grammatical Man,* 152.
30. Weaver, "The Search for Our Ancestors," 614.
31. Eiseley, *The Firmament of Time,* 113.
32. Weaver, "The Search for Our Anestors," 615
33. Campbell, *Grammatical Man,* 153.
34. G. K. Chesterton, *The Everlasting Man* (Garden City, N.Y.: Doubleday, 1955), 28.
35. John N. Wilford, "Artistry of the Ice Age," *New York Times Magazine,* 12 October 1986, p. 54.
36. Campbell, *Grammatical Man,* 154.
37. Ibid., 153–56.
38. Bruce Bower, "When the Human Spirit Soared," *Science News* 130 (1986): 378–79.
39. Richard Dawkins, *The Selfish Gene* (Oxford: Oxford University Press, 1976).
40. Ibid., 21, 22.
41. Edward O. Wilson, *Sociobiology: The New Synthesis* (Cambridge: Belknap Press, Harvard University Press, 1975). See also a recent extension of these ideas: Charles J. Lumsden and Edward O. Wilson, *Genes, Mind and Culture: The Coevolutionary Process* (Cambridge: Harvard University Press, 1981).
42. Charles B. Thaxton, William L. Bradley, and R. L. Olsen, *The Mystery of Life's Origin: Reassessing Current Theories* (New York: Philosophical Library, 1984). See also P. T. Mora, "Reductionist Myth and Holistic Metaphysics in Biology," in *New Approaches to Genetics,* ed. P. W. Kent (Stocksfield, U.K.: Oriel Press, 1978), 234–43.
43. R. C. Lewontin, Steven Rose, and Leon J. Kamin, *Not in Our Genes* (New York: Pantheon, 1984), 236–37.
44. Loren Eiseley, *The Unexpected Universe,* 77–78.
45. Ibid., 71–72.
46. Ibid., 87, 91.
47. Genesis 1:1–26.
48. Genesis 1:26–27.
49. Genesis 2:7.
50. Arthur R. Peacocke, *Creation and the World of Science* (Oxford: Clarendon Press, 1979), 137–46.
51. Ibid., 145.
52. John 1:1–3, NEB.
53. Heb. 1:3, KJV.
54. John 1:14, 29.
55. Pierre Tielhard de Chardin, *Science and Christ* (London: Collins, 1968), 167.
56. Arden Almquist, "Ode to a Pet Chimpanzee," *The Covenant Companion,* July 1985.
57. Philippians 2:5–8.
58. John 7:46.

9. Mysteries Multiplied

HISTORICAL PERSPECTIVE

The Tangible Becomes Illusion

In past chapters we have tried to portray the impact of modern scientific discovery upon our understanding of ourselves and our place in the created universe. What punctuates the analysis repeatedly is that there is a grand design and an even grander Designer. To see it otherwise is to ignore a trend—most obvious within the past century—toward seeing increasing complexity and multiplying mystery within the entire body of science. Anthropologist Loren Eiseley describes the phenomenon in his book *The Firmament of Time:*

A scientist writing around the turn of the century remarked that all of the past generations of men have lived and died in a world of illusions. The unconscious irony in his observation consists in the fact that this man assumed the progress of science to have been so great that a clear vision of the world without illusion was, by his own time, possible. It is needless to add that he wrote before Einstein, before the spread of Freud's doctrines, at a time when Mendel was just about to be rediscovered, and before advances in the study of radioactivity had made their impact—of both illumination and confusion—upon this century.

Certainly science has moved forward. But when science progresses, it often opens vaster mysteries to our gaze. Moreover, science frequently discovers that it must abandon or modify what it once believed. Sometimes it ends by accepting what it has previously scorned. The simplistic idea that science marches undeviatingly down an ever broadening highway can scarcely be sustained by the historian of ideas.[1]

Progress is always attended by the correction of error, by sharp shifts in direction and emphasis. And the nature of the correction is again only tentative, only partially truth, yet it proves to be tremendously fruitful. And the illusions could hardly be said to have been dispelled. In fact, in a very real sense, what we have started with as the tangible—matter, energy, space, and time— now seems to bear some of the mystery of an illusion. Certainly, things are not what they seemed. In the words of science writer K. C. Cole:

So much of science consists of things we can never see: light "waves" and charged "particles"; magnetic "fields" and gravitational "forces"; quantum "jumps" and electron "orbits." In fact, none of these phenomena is literally what we say it is. Light waves do not undulate through empty space in the same way that water waves ripple over a still pond; a field is only a mathematical description of the strength and direction of a force; an atom does not literally jump from one quantum state to another, and electrons do not really travel around the atomic nucleus in orbits. The words we use are merely metaphors. "When it comes to atoms," wrote Niels Bohr, "language can be used only as in poetry. The poet, too, is not nearly so concerned with describing facts as with creating images."[2]

It may seem curious that humans, made in the image of God, should turn out to be image-makers themselves, even at the level of science. But this is of necessity, for the descriptions we use for that which is essentially unseeable must be made of the seeable world we experience every day.

THE MULTIPLICATION OF COMPLEXITY

Physics has brought us some of the most fascinating developments in science. Astrophysicist Michael Shallis, in his book *On Time,* reminds us that Heisenberg's uncertainty principle limited our precision of measurement of interdependent quantities such as the position and motion of elementary particles. That is, precision in the measurement of position can be gained only at the expense of losing information about velocity. There can be no absolute certainty at the subatomic level.[3]

But Shallis goes on to point out that, in addition to position and velocity, the uncertainty principle operates for two other properties: energy and time. This is because the limit of uncertainty must always exceed the value of Planck's constant, 10^{-34} Joule seconds, the size of one unit of action. If a physicist wishes to gain knowledge of the energy of a subatomic force, for example, he or she must sacrifice the accuracy of measurement of the time interval over which the force operates.

These limitations in the measurement of the behavior of subatomic particles require that any description be restricted to statistical methods. As Shallis says,

Quantum theory is a probabilistic description of nature, not as in the macroscopic world because of the sheer numbers of particles, but because of an inherent property of indeterminism in describing physical reality. This final restriction on the attainability of absolute knowledge has worried many scientists, but the current consensus is that the quantum theory is the fundamental theory of nature.[4]

But the sheer number of subatomic particles discovered by physicists in the past few years is another example of the remarkable increase in the complexity of our descriptions of nature. Experimenters have found a whole range of new "fundamental particles," upward of two hundred in number, more than double the number of known distinct atoms of the elements once thought to be the fundamental building blocks of matter. Most exist for only a fraction of a second, as part of subatomic interactions, and most have also been demonstrated to have an opposite number, an "antiparticle" of opposite charge, a sort of mirror image of themselves.

This increase in complexity, with no final simplification, for which scientists have always searched, seems to be the nature of things in every field. It was also seen for the case of molecular genetics in Chapter 5. This suggests that there are limitations in our ability to comprehend the universe in the familiar terms of matter, energy, space, and time. Perhaps these are but the explicit manifestations of a more fundamental order. That order can be looked at as a holistic, implicate order, which refuses to be divided, as David Bohm suggests[5] (discussed in Chapter 6), or, in the ultimate sense, as the immanent, active participation of the Creator, "who holds in being the whole universe" as part of his own ultimate reality.[6]

THE ACCELERATION OF DISCOVERY

The increase in complexity of scientific descriptions has been accompanied by an acceleration in the rate of scientific progress. Astronomer Gerald Hawkins, in his book *Mindsteps to the Cosmos,* sees progress in terms of great breakthroughs in thought, at first widely separated, but becoming more frequent as history unfolds.[7] His is an astronomical perspective, delineating the progress of thought in terms of steps in humankind's comprehension of the universe. He proposes that the first great "mindstep" occurred when humans drew their first pictures in caves, thirty thousand to forty thousand years ago. This was the "threshold of cosmic awareness." Hawkins argues that Sapiens modern took over from Sapiens neandertal and added the dimension of cosmic thought. The Neandertals had developed considerable human skill, including a spoken language of sorts, and a knowledge of plants and game, of clouds and weather. They had even, as we discussed in Chapter 8, displayed compassion for the sick and respect for the dead. But, Hawkins says, they had not *looked up.* The first evidence of an interest in the sky was in the drawings found in a cave in the farm of La Pileta, in southern Spain. Here the artist had drawn, with pigments made from water, fat, and minerals, pictures of animals, mysterious symbols, and circles with rays, which surely represented the sun. The symbols seemed to Hawkins to have astronomical significance, depicting numbers related to the movements of perhaps sun and moon.

Writing first appeared in the form of tablets bearing pictures and symbols in ancient Mesopotamia (present-day Iraq, Iran, and Jordan) at about 8000 B.C. The first story ever written, called the epic of Gilgamesh, was recorded on twelve clay tablets dating back to 2700 B.C. It is a story within a story, in which the human players are acting out a human drama, but also illustrating the phases of the moon and its relationship to the sun. This Hawkins suggests as the next great mindstep, that of myth and legend, with the sun, moon, and stars as participants, sometimes with occult powers of their own. Contemporary with the Gilgamesh epic was the practice, in ancient Britain, of building with large stones: megaliths. The site at Stonehenge is particularly interesting, in that there is again the strong correlation with astronomical movements. Arrangements of these massive stones were made to measure movements of the sun and moon. These developments were soon followed by other writings describing the worship of the planet Venus, the morning star. One version comes from Babylon, in the Old World, and the second, somewhat later, from the Mayan empire, in the New World.

The next great mindstep, by Hawkins's reckoning, occurred in 150 A.D., contemporary with the life and work of Ptolemy the astronomer. Ptolemy lived and worked in Alexandria, taking advantage of the greatest library in the ancient world. His great contribution was the demonstration of astronomical order: the orderly motion of the planets. This was also the age of mathematics, and it ushered in a period of great astronomical study, much of it by Arab astronomers and mathematicians.

The next mindstep is attributed to Copernicus, the Polish canon who spent a lifetime analyzing the movement of the sun and planets, and concluded that the Earth orbits the sun and also spins on its axis. Although his work was almost lost, and the eventual publication, *De Revolutionibus,* was censored by the church, the path was laid for a true revolution in thinking of the relation of humankind to the cosmos. This mindstep is dated at 1543 A.D., the year of publication of Copernicus's work.

The last mindstep is set at the onset of the space age, in 1926, when Robert Goddard launched the first liquid-fuel rocket. The pace of discovery that this ushered in is almost unbelievable, with human travel to the moon and unmanned space vehicle exploration of almost all the other planets of our solar system following.

But what is most intriguing is the timing of these five steps. The interval has been shortening drastically. The interval of time between the cave drawings and the Gilgamesh epic is approximately 30,000 years. The next interval, between Gilgamesh and the age of mathematics and Ptolemy's ordering of the planets, is 2850 years. Between Ptolemy and Copernicus is 1393 years, and from Coopernicus to the space age is 383 years.

The implication of this analysis is that scientific progress, as seen in humankind's understanding of the cosmos, has been accelerating rapidly, and that we may expect wholly new perceptions to burst upon our understanding in rapid succession. By Hawkins's calculation we should have additional astronomical breakthroughs in the years 2021, 2045, and 2051. Beyond that point progress could be viewed as almost exponential.

An interesting corollary of this analysis is that each mindstep has been attended by a technological breakthrough. The first step coincides with the paintbrush, the second with the pen, the third with the development of mathematics, the fourth with printing, and the last with the computer. The linkage between the human mind and its mechanical appendages is tight. Hawkins further suggests that, because all these mindsteps have been accomplished by breakthroughs in communication, we might expect the next mindstep to coincide with another communication breakthrough—perhaps with extraterrestrial intelligence. Finally, in a fascinating concluding chapter to his book, Hawkins speculates on the next mindstep:

Mindstep 6 could be proof, the demonstration of the existence of something unseen, a new type of field connected with life, the existence of which is so persuasive that its general acceptance is inevitable. In religious contexts it could be identified with the world of the spirit. In this area there are scientific indicators which may or may not be precursors. There are the broad questions of telepathy, existence or not of a vital force, the existence of the soul, and continuation of life after death. Then there are the unmeasurable human emotions of love, friendship and hate, pleasure and pain. Are these all interlocking parts of a non-physical cosmos? The atoms of iron and carbon in the body, made in the core of stars, will ultimately be returned to the cosmos, but thoughts and brain waves go without leaving a trace. These things cannot be seen through the microscope or radio telescope, yet they are things that humans are made of.[8]

It seems clear that we can expect the pace of scientific progress to continue at an ever-increasing rate, bringing with it new and undreamed-of perspectives for the future.

EXAMPLES OF THE DEEPENING MYSTERY

Wondrous Shapes in Heaven and on Earth

In January of 1987, astronomer Roger Lynds of Kitt Peak National Observatory reported that he had found two and possibly three bright, luminous arcs stretching between galaxies in three of the fifty-eight galaxies he had examined. The discovery was unprecedented, these objects being the largest continuous structures ever observed. They are more than 300,000 light years long, blue, sharply defined, and formed in almost perfect circular arcs. Their luminosity is equal to 100 billion suns. Lynds and coworker-theoretician Vahe Petrosian of Stanford think the arcs are made up of masses of young stars, and that they may represent some kind of propagating shock front from the interior of a cluster of nearby galaxies. Perhaps they represent an early step in the evolution of galaxy clusters, because Lynds has noted that they occur at great distances, which means that we are observing them at a young age. Indeed, one of the arcs reveals some nodules along its length, as if it were beginning to break up into clumps about the size of small galaxies.[9]

About a year earlier, a trio of astronomers, Valerie de Lapparent, of the University of Paris, and Margaret Geller and John Huchra, both of the Harvard-Smithsonian Center for Astrophysics, had reported their observations of a slice of the universe. They found the galaxies to be arranged in long, curving chains oriented about huge cavities almost free of matter. The galaxies are, so to speak, arranged along the walls of giant bubbles.[10] These arcs and bubbles are two of the most recently discovered visible shapes in the heavens, and they tell us that there is more structure to the expanding universe than we had supposed.

Among the most mysterious objects in the heavens are a type of galaxies referred to as "active." Here we enter a world of violence. Certain types of galaxies, Harding Smith tells us in his article in a book entitled *The Universe,* exhibit stunning explosive events in or near their centers, which overshadow the energy produced by their multitudes of stars.[11] These "explosive galaxies" dwarf a normal galaxy's energy production by factors of hundreds of thousands or more. Among the most interesting and mysterious objects in this category are the so-called radio stars, powerful energy sources distributed around the sky. Astronomers dubbed them quasistellar radio sources or simply quasars. Actually most quasars are not radio stars, but the energy they all emit is staggering. One theory for their energy sources is the continuous explosion of supernovae at their centers. Another and presently more popular theory invokes black holes, places in galaxies where gravity is so strong that nothing, not even light, can escape. The energy of a black hole, believed to be derived from gravitational collapse, must be enormous, for there is strong evidence that they are small by galactic standards. Astronomer William Kaufmann explains in *The Universe,*

Active galaxies and quasars exhibit surprisingly rapid brightness fluctuations. They flare up and dim back down over periods as short as a week. The frequency of such variations is related to the size of the object. Since nothing can travel faster than the speed of light, an object cannot fluctuate in brightness faster than light travels across that object. For instance, an object one light-year in diameter cannot fluctuate in brightness faster than once a year. Since quasars and active galaxies fluctuate as rapidly as once a week, their energy-producing regions must be as small as one light-week in diameter. Thus quasars and active galaxies produce the brightness of a hundred galaxies from a region roughly the size of the solar system!

How can so much energy be created in such a small volume? That has been a thorny question for astrophysicists since the 1960's. The answer seems to involve exceedingly massive black holes, each typically containing as much matter as a billion Suns. If a so-called supermassive black hole exists at the center of a galaxy, it would certainly attract enormous amounts of interstellar gas and dust. As the in-falling material plunges toward the hole, it would become extremely hot and release the huge energy output that astronomers observe. In a seeming paradox, therefore, black holes are responsible for the most luminous objects in the universe.[12]

And, as if arcs and bubbles and black holes were not enough, along comes the string theory, a theory that demands the addition of six additional dimensions beyond the usual four: height, breadth, width, and time. K. C. Cole, in a *New York Times Magazine* article, elaborates:

"String Theory," as it is commonly known (some scientists call it "super-string theory"), does away with the familiar image of a universe composed of billiard-ball-like particles pushed and pulled by familiar forces like gravity and electricity. Quantum theory had already revealed in the 1920's that the billiard balls have curious wave-like properties: they are more like vibrations than well-defined points in space. Now string theory is proposing that these points, in fact, are tiny loops, or closed "strings," that the universe is built not of Grape-Nuts but of Cheerios. The strings, too, vibrate invisibly in subtle resonances. These vibrations, so the theory goes, make up everything in the universe—from light to lightning bugs, from gravity to gold.

These strings are not, of course, visible, nor are they like rubber bands or pieces of twine. Impossible to detect by any means known to science today, they are mathematical curves. Talking about strings, like talking about billiard balls or waves, is a crude way of trying to comprehend the unfamiliar in familiar terms. But then, physics has always had to resort to metaphor.[13]

The leading proponent of the string theory is a Princeton physicist now at the neighboring Institute for Advanced Study. His name is Edward Witten, and he enjoys challenges. Indeed, some of the mathematics necessary to handle the string theory has yet to be invented. But, as Cole explains, "For Witten, String Theory is too good not to be true," and Witten adds that the string theory is "a piece of 21st-century physics that fell by chance in the 20th century." What physicists are working with today is but "a few crumbs from the table compared to the feast that awaits us."[14]

The Elusive Nature of Time

Asymmetry: The Seven Arrows of Time

Time is a concept we live with daily and yet hardly understand. As Tony Rothman put it,

You can't see time, you can't hear it or taste it, and while you may have a lot on your hands, before you know it, time runs out. We all know that time flies, unless it stands still. We can measure it, yet even when we turn back the clock, time marches on.[15]

We all agree that time marches on, that it has direction, that the future is ahead. This is one of the fundamental aspects of our existence. Rothman calls it psychological time, one of seven kinds of time for which there appears to be no reversibility, no symmetry. Curiously, according to Oxford cosmologist Roger Penrose, none of these "arrows of time" is explainable by physics. In the world of Isaac Newton, the science of mechanics, everything was idealized as billiard balls: planets were large billiard balls, water and air were made up of microscopic billiard balls. In mechanics there is no arrow of time built in: every event that mechanics describes is reversible. The motion of the planets could be clockwise or counterclockwise, and Newton's equations would be the same. If that were true for us human beings, obeying the time-reversible rules of Newton, why shouldn't the future be as accessible to our memory as is the past? In the white Queen's words to Alice, "It's a poor sort of memory that only works backward." Perhaps there *is* some kind of reversibility here, but it would defy the everyday experience of most of us.

The second anomalous time in Penrose's list is the radiation arrow of time. As Maxwell has shown us, in his laws of electromagnetism, radiation is always propagated in one direction, outward from the source. The fact that waves do not return to the source is the second instance of irreversibility.

The third of time's irreversibilities is in quantum mechanics, in one small but fundamental aspect: the crucial instant when the observation is made. At the point of observation, Penrose tells us, there is no obvious way for a reversal of the result.

The fourth arrow of time is related to the decay of a subatomic particle called a kaon. In 1964 two Princeton physicists, Val Fitch and James Cronin, showed that, contrary to the assumption that particle decay proceeded at the same rate whether time ran forward or backward, this assumption of reversibility was not true, at least for kaons. Physicist Tony Rothman explains:

Fitch and Cronin couldn't reverse time directly, of course; all the arrows we've dealt with so far suggest that that would be difficult, if not impossible. But they did the next best thing. According to a famous theorem from quantum mechanics, called CPT for charge-parity-time, if we take our world, change all the matter into anti-matter (i.e., reverse its atomic charge), reflect it into a mirror (change its parity) and run time backward, the result should be a world indistinguishable from the one we started with. But when Fitch and Cronin reversed two of the three CPT features—charge and parity—some kaons decayed at a rate slightly different from normal. That implied that the decay rate in a time-inverted world would be different too. (The reasoning is tricky. It's analogous to a situation in which you have three numbers—C, P, and T—that equal some constant: if you change the value of C times P, then you must change the value of T as well to make sure their product will remain the same.)

Nature is being very subtle here. Only in the neutral kaon does she reveal the fourth arrow of time. Uranium, thorium, radon, etc., all decay at rates independent of time's direction. Is the kaon's behavior an accident, a minor welding defect in God's construction of the universe? Physicists don't like accidents. As E. C. G. Sudarshan, the master of metaphor who first investigated tachyons, has said, "It's like a grain of sand in an oyster—small, but you can't ignore it." The scientific community hasn't ignored it: Fitch and Cronin were awarded the 1980 Nobel Prize in physics.[16]

The last three arrows of time are more speculative, yet nonetheless fascinating in their philosophical implications. Arrow five arises from the distinction between black holes and their hypothetical counterpart, "white holes." White holes began as a facetious idea, by Penrose, that if a black hole were turned upside down, it would become a white hole. One consequence of the inversion would be that time would run in reverse. But that possibility creates difficulties for a number of reasons. For example, black holes are the consequence of the collapse of massive stars into objects so dense that even light can't escape their intense gravitational field. Running the picture backward, to yield white holes, we would expect sudden explosions in the universe in which ordinary matter was created in vast quantities. None have been found. For this and because of other implausible expectations, it is concluded that white holes are forbidden. Hence we have another irreversibility, another arrow of time.

Penrose attributed arrow six to the expectation that time, which is of course unidirectional in the expanding universe, would also maintain its direction if the universe stopped expanding and began to collapse back toward its original singularity. Some physicists, notably Stephen Hawking of Cambridge, have argued until recently, on the basis of the highly ordered nature of matter near a singularity, that time would be reversed during the collapse. The results of such a process would be strange indeed! Trees would "ungrow," broken crockery would reassemble, corrosion would reverse, shattered watches would come together in working order again, mountains would build up rather than erode, and we would all be engaged in backpedaling. The implications are so absurd that we know something is wrong! Recall, too, that in our discussion of order, in Chapter 6, we noted that Ilya Prigogine has shown irreversibility in thermodynamic processes to be so pervasive that it must be built in at a fundamental level.

Hawking has recently reversed his position, based upon new theoretical approaches to the origin of the universe, which make the expansion and contraction phases very different.[17] So there is agreement that, should there be a collapse of the universe, time will not reverse. Another arrow of time!

Much of what has been in view in terms of this consideration of irreversibility in an expanding and contracting universe relates to entropy, that measure of disorder which the second law of thermodynamics tells us always increases in a system undergoing change. Recall that thermodynamicists had shown that entropy is responsible for the inefficiency in energy transformation, because it represents the amount of energy converted to an unusable form, which is related to the increased molecular disorder of a system. The upshot of the second law is that systems always move toward a condition of increased entropy, or disorder. And this is Penrose's seventh arrow of time.

But the schism between the reversibility of mechanics and the irreversibility of thermodynamics remains. Many leading physicists still treat entropy as an accident of statistics, stating that only in a system with a large number of objects does entropy increase. In response, Prigogine argues that there are intrinsically random systems that display an increase in entropy regardless of how few particles are present. Physicist Rothman concludes with words of hope:

Yet neither thermodynamicists nor cosmologists have satisfactorily explained time's seven arrows. It may well be that many, if not all, are linked in ways not yet clearly understood. Someday the realms of the reversible and the irreversible may be joined, the schism between the followers of Newton and the followers of Boltzmann mended, and the riddle of time resolved. The day may be far off. But let us not lose hope. There's plenty of time.[18]

Virtual Particles: A Subatomic Perspective on Time

Physicists refer to the force that holds the atomic nucleus together as the strong force, but the way this force acts between subatomic particles is a nagging problem. For that matter, any force that operates at a distance—gravitation and electromagnetism are other examples—has always seemed unsatisfactory to scientists. Recently the explanation for subatomic interactions has taken a more mechanistic but surprising turn, based upon the operation of what are called exchange, or virtual particles. The first example Michael Shallis tells us about in his book *On Time* is an exchange between two electrons, which mutually repel each other by the mechanism of exchanging a photon.[19] In a sense the electron throws the photon at another electron, which catches it, with a resultant exchange of energy and change in direction. It is as though two skaters were tossing a heavy ball back and forth. When one skater throws the ball he recoils from the throw and changes direction on the ice, just as does the skater who catches the ball. The only additional feature is that the interaction involves many exchanges: the ball is traded back and forth many times during the interaction.

The mysterious questions here relate to the source of the exchange particles and the timing of their exchange. Shallis calls our attention to another exchange process, the mutual repulsion of two protons, which is mediated by the exchange of an elementary particle called a pi-meson. The pi-meson has a mass one-seventh that of the proton, and the exchange of this large mass explains the strength of the internuclear force. The source of this pi-meson is explained with the help of Heisenberg's uncertainty principle. Earlier in this chapter we mentioned that the uncertainty at the elementary particle level not only operates for its position and velocity, but also for a second pair of properties: energy and time. That is, the product of the uncertainty in energy multiplied by the uncertainty in time must be greater than a particular small number. Now, if the time element in this relationship is small enough, then the energy involved can be as large as necessary. Because Einstein has shown, through his theory of special relativity, that energy and mass are equivalent, the mass required for the creation of an exchange particle could be obtained by the conversion of energy into mass, provided the process occurs rapidly enough. Once again, time is the key. As Shallis says,

A proton can produce a pion (pi-meson) out of the uncertainty in its energy/time budget provided it does so for a very short time only. Indeed when time intervals become short enough almost anything can happen; matter can be created, forces occur and so on.[20]

Because of the brevity of their existence, exchange particles are often called virtual particles. The more massive the virtual particle, the shorter the time interval and the closer the emitting particles must be to each other. This explains why the strong nuclear force operates over only short distances, because the exchange particles must be massive, whereas in the case of the electromagnetic force, the distances are greater, because the photon is massless and so requires little energy for its creation.

The question of the decision as to the timing of exchanges of virtual particles has an intriguing answer: they are being created and destroyed all the time. As Shallis describes the phenomenon:

Although particle interactions or forces are due to the exchange of virtual particles, there is nothing in quantum theory to prevent virtual particles from being created at any time, providing they do not exist for long. A proton might be found on its own emitting a pion and then reabsorbing it, and indeed any such virtual particle creation that can be imagined can in practice occur, and does occur, within the rules of quantum probability. Instead of imagining particles like protons sedately moving along, a more realistic picture would be that they are surrounded by a haze of seething virtual particles, none of which exist for more than vanishingly small times. Such a particle, when approached by another, does not need to "know" a repulsion is required; the cloud of virtual particles will overlap and particle exchange will occur.[21]

The picture we use to describe subatomic particles and the forces acting between them seems to have a kind of mechanistic explanation, but it is a bizarre one. The mysteries continue to multiply!

Time and Aging: Relativistic Time

In Chapter 3 we discussed the contribution of Einstein's theory of special relativity to our understanding of the universe. Its most startling conclusion was that two events that occur at the same instant for one observer may not be simultaneous for another observer if the two are moving rapidly relative to each other. The crucial thing in relativity is that light has the same speed regardless of who measures it, as first shown by physicist Albert Michelson in 1881. This is because light is a vibration of pure energy, rather than a material substance. As Alan Lightman describes it in his article "Relativity for the Table," this result seems odd because it had been naturally assumed that light traveled in some material medium, in which case its measured speed would vary with a change in motion of the observer, the so-called Doppler effect.[22] We are all familiar with what happens when you approach a train or automobile whose horn is blowing. The pitch lowers as soon as you pass. Why does it not hold true for light? The difference with light is strange. For example, you know that if you walk on a moving escalator, you'll arrive sooner than if you stand. And if a light beam passes between two people, one walking toward its source and one standing still, common sense tells you that the beam would pass the moving person faster than the stationary one. Actually, each sees the beam going by *at the same speed.*

To illustrate the phenomenon, Lightman gives us a version of one of Einstein's own examples:

Imagine a train traveling through the countryside. In one of the cars a person sets up a screen exactly in the center of the car and a light bulb at either end of the car. The screen is wired so that if it is illuminated on both sides at precisely the same instant, a bell rings. (Our traveler has brought along some fancy equipment.) The car is now darkened, and the person arranges to turn on both lights simultaneously. He can verify these two events happened simultaneously because the bell rings. Since the two light beams traveled the same distance to get to the screen, halfway down the car, and traveled with the same speed, they had to have been emitted from their bulbs at the same instant. Now let's analyze this experiment from my perspective, as I stand outside beside the tracks. I, of course, also hear the bell ring. A ringing bell undeniably signals that the two light beams struck the screen simultaneously. Prior to this, however, I observed the two light beams were emitted at different times, for the following reason: I saw one light beam traveling in the same direction as the train and one in the opposite direction. The first beam had to travel farther than half a car length before striking the screen, because during its time of transit the train moved forward a bit. The second beam traveled less. Since both beams have the same speed for me as well as for the man in the train (remember, the speed of light is independent of the motion of the source or observer) the first beam had to have been emitted slightly before the second. For ordinary train speeds and lengths, this delay would be something like one-hundredth of one-trillionth of a second—hardly noticeable, but detectable by highly precise clocks. While clocks in the train would show the two light beams traveled precisely the same length of time, clocks on the ground would not. The concept of simultaneity is not absolute, as it seems, but relative to the motion of the observer.

These kinds of discrepancies get bigger as the relative velocity between the two observers increases. If the train were not moving at all relative to me, the fellow on the train and I would agree exactly on everything having to do with time. At the other extreme, if the train were moving by me at almost the speed of light, the first beam would travel a great distance before reaching the screen and the other beam practically not at all, so that the two events of emission, from my frame of reference, would be widely separated in time.

You might at this point be willing to admit that odd things happen when light is involved, but otherwise prefer to stick with your common sense. However, in my illustration light served only as a convenient tool for measuring time. The emission of light at the two ends of the train car could be the herald of any two events in those locations. The birth of two babies, for example, in which case different observers would disagree on whether the babies were born at the same time.[23]

It is time, then, that is curiously different for different observers, depending on their motion relative to each other.

Perhaps the most bizarre example of this effect is provided by Michael Shallis, for the case of a hypothetical spaceship journey at velocities approaching the speed of light. Here, an additional aspect is provided by the presence of acceleration, which introduces an asymmetry into the picture and allows for the two observers to see the differences in time:

Imagine that a fifty year old man and his twenty-five year old daughter each have their twin atomic clocks. The father and his clock get in a rocket which accelerates at ten metres per second every second. This acceleration is equal to the acceleration due to gravity on earth, so this travelling man feels quite at home in his rocket with what appears to him to be terrestrial conditions. He keeps his rocket engine firing for a month, by which time he will have gained a speed, with respect to the earth, of close to ninety percent of the speed of light. At the end of the month the rocket is turned around, subjecting the father to a little momentary discomfort, but the engines are kept blazing and the craft decelerates until at the end of the second month it is at rest with respect to the earth. The rockets keep burning and the craft accelerates back towards home for another month, when again it is travelling at about nine-tenths of the speed of light. Again, it is reversed so that for the final month of the journey it is slowing down and lands back on earth. The father checks his atomic clock and assures himself that his journey has taken him exactly four months. He opens up the door of the rocket and there is an elderly woman to greet him.

"Father," she cries, "how wonderful to see you!" The man's daughter is now sixty years old, ten years older than her father, for time ran more slowly in the rocket than it did on earth, and the stay-at-home atomic clock has ticked its way through thirty-five years. As far as the daughter was concerned the father travelled to a distance of about fifteen light years away and didn't send a signal that he was on his way home until she was in her fifties.[24]

This, of course, is a hypothetical case, since it is not possible at present to attain such speeds, but the effect has been verified by flying very precise atomic clocks around the world in airplanes. It even affected the astronauts who went to the moon in 1969. Shallis tells us that on their return they had aged five thousand millionths of a second less than their spouses, who had stayed at home.

THE MYSTERY OF HUMAN CONSCIOUSNESS

In his Gifford lectures of 1977–78, Nobel laureate Sir John Eccles sets forth as his aim "to review the sense of wonder and mystery in our human existence."[25] His early task is to review the big bang, then he recounts the remarkable cosmic evolution leading to life forms, and finally he reviews the development of conscious, intelligent human beings. For Eccles the evolutionary explanation, as it is normally presented, guided by chance and uninfluenced by any existing need, fails in one important aspect: it cannot account for the existence of each one of us as unique, self-conscious human beings. There is about biological evolution, he says, a "strange waywardness," which led to the highly improbable—intelligent life—in the same mysterious way that cosmic evolution was somehow biased toward the origin of life, the so-called anthropic principle we considered in Chapter 4.

In the advent of human beings, there was a sharp division, a sudden bifurcation in which biological evolution was joined by a new phenomenon, cultural evolution. Primitive humankind had acquired, at the expense of some limitation of the sensory capabilities, a brain of sufficient complexity for communication by language. From this crucial point on, brain and culture developed together over half a million years; in the process the brain size increased threefold, and culture supplied the evolutionary selection pressure for the quality of that increase.

But Eccles tells us that, in addition to the rich world of culture, there also developed another uniquely human phenomenon, that of self-consciousness, or self-awareness. In their book *The Wonder of Being Human,* Eccles and Daniel Robinson elaborate on this special human capacity.[26] Self-consciousness implies knowing that you know, and it is authenticated by the fact that other human beings share in this experience. To account for this unique development, Eccles and Robinson propose that the subjective world of consciousness characteristic of mammalian species was drastically changed by the addition of a new element, which he calls the psyche, the self, or the soul. It is argued that this new capability also developed in a progressive manner, from faint self-awareness in the pre-Neanderthals to abstract thought and agape love as representative modern human capabilities or at least potentialities.

This development of humankind is paralleled in the way a child develops progressively from the consciousness of the baby to the self-awareness of the child. The life of the baby is certainly a conscious one, with a great variety of emotional states: happiness, excitement, fear, anger, frustration, pleasure, pain. The first learning tasks of the baby are concurrent with its recognition of spatial relations in a visual world. Eccles and Robinson point out that this begins with "hand viewing," which by about five months has led to the skill of grasping objects. A parallel learning program is mediated by crawling. It is interesting that even these familiar experiences defy full explanation. As Eccles and Robinson expressed it,

In this way each of us has learned to interpret the sensory inputs from the retinal images, which from moment to moment give us the world that we can move in with assurance. In a manner that we do not understand, the baby learns to use its brain in order to bring about the movements that it desires. Throughout life we continue to develop this conscious control of our brains in bringing about voluntary movements but it is, in its essentials, an utterly mysterious process.[27]

Complementing the visual-spatial learning program of the baby is the development of language. Long before recognizable words are uttered, the baby is experimenting incessantly with the articulation of phonemes, which will eventually find expression in the first words: Mama, Papa, and so on. The process involves learning complex muscle movements of larynx, pharynx, tongue, mouth, lungs, and diaphragm. It is a process of which the chimpanzee is incapable. Apparently the chimp can make a variety of noises, but does not have a brain capable of learning the motor programs required for speech.

The baby's accomplishments to this point are remarkable. But the next steps in development are transcendent. At eighteen months the child recognizes itself in a mirror and begins to use speech for a different purpose, to ask questions about itself and about the world outside itself. It is a graduation into childhood as a participant in the wider world. He or she has moved from the limited conscious life of the baby to the self-conscious life of the human child.

Eccles and Robinson suggest that this progressive development from the consciousness of the baby to the self-consciousness of the child provides a good model for the emergence of self-consciousness in early humankind. In Chapter 8 we discussed the sudden appearance of the large-brained Homo neandertal, and noted that with their advent, 150,000 years ago, there occurred an enormous acceleration in cultural development. But paralleling this development, and early in their history, Neandertal displayed a hitherto unseen characteristic among the genus Homo, that of caring. Neandertals cared for their dead, providing flowers for the burial and including implements and protective grave structures, with a view to a future life. They also looked after their sick, evidenced by the discovery of 60,000-year-old skeletons of two severely incapacitated Neandertals who had been extensively cared for by other tribe members.

This outward view, this view beyond the self, carried over into the themes for artistic expression presented so exquisitely in the caves of early humans. There was portrayed here a love of nature, a desire to record the animals of the field and the mysterious lights in the heavens. As noted earlier in this chapter, the look upward to the heavens was a unique part of the human odyssey, another step in the development of humankind's sense of the transcendent, utterly beyond self and even other humans: a look toward the Divine. Here, then, in this developmental process, came about a radically new experience for evolving life. Humankind had arrived not just at a point of sophistication in toolmaking and artistry, but early men and women had found their inner selves and each other as worthy subjects for love and care. And beyond this, they had found some sense of value and purpose that transcended their immediate lives, a destiny beyond the grave, which otherwise only provoked a new kind of fear.

The mystery of the origin of self-awareness is remarked upon by some of the keenest intellects of recent times. Eccles and Robinson quote from geneticist T. Dobzhansky:

Self-awareness is, then, one of the fundamental, possibly the most fundamental, characteristic of the human species. This characteristic is an evolutionary novelty; the biological species from which mankind has descended had only rudiments of self-awareness, or perhaps lacked it altogether.[28]

They also note philosopher Karl Popper's words:

The emergence of all consciousness, capable of self-reflection, is indeed one of the greatest of miracles.[29]

Finally, they recall animal behaviorist Konrad Lorenz's reference to self-awareness as

that most mysterious of barriers, utterly impenetrable to the human understanding, that runs through the middle of what is the undeniable oneness of our personality—the barrier that divides our subjective experience from the objective, verifiable physiological events that occur in our body.[30]

Nowhere in the natural sciences is there an explanation for the emergence of this strange, nonmaterial entity called self-consciousness, or mind. Perhaps this is also why the mind is relegated to a passive role in the way many philosophers and neuroscientists explain brain function. By contrast, Eccles and Robinson propose a "dualist-interactionist" explanation in which mind and brain are independent entities that somehow interact.[31] The interaction of the nonmaterial mind and the material brain occurs by way of the flow of information, not of energy. Thus the world of matter-energy is not completely sealed, as physicists generally hold, but contains small apertures for the transfer of information between the seat of self-awareness and the brain itself. This proposal, coming from one of the world's greatest neuroscientists, leads us to the conclusion that brain physiology now begins to look as open-ended and indeterminate as cosmology or quantum physics. Once more we enter the unknown!

In the last section of their book, Eccles and Robinson leave us with one stirring admonition:

The principal trouble with mankind today is that the intellectual leaders are too arrogant in their self-sufficiency. We must realize the great unknowns in the material makeup and operation of our brains, in the relationship of brain to mind, in our creative imagination, and in the uniqueness of the psyche. When we think of these unknowns as well as the unknown of how we come to be in the first place, we should be much more humble.[32]

The multiplied mysteries that confront us in the universe, in the subatomic world, and in ourselves should bring us, not to a posture of arrogance and pride, but rather to our knees before the great God of the universe, who has spoken this vast and fascinating cosmos into being.

NOTES

1. Loren Eiseley, *The Firmament of Time* (New York: Atheneum, 1984), 5.
2. K. C. Cole, "On Imagining the Unseeable," *Discover,* December 1982, 70.
3. Michael Shallis, *On Time* (New York: Schocken Books, 1983), 74–75.
4. Shallis, *On Time,* 75.
5. David Bohm, *Wholeness and the Implicate Order* (London: Routledge and Kegan Paul, 1980).
6. Heb. 1:3, paraphrased by Donald M. MacKay.
7. Gerald Hawkins, *Mindsteps to the Cosmos* (New York: Harper & Row, 1983).
8. Hawkins, *Mindsteps to the Cosmos,* 307–8.
9. Mitchell Waldrop, "Luminous Arcs Dwarf the Galaxies," *Science News* 131 (1987): 22.
10. Dietrick Thomsen, "Strings That Blow Bubbles in the Cosmos," *Science News* 131 (1987): 22.
11. Harding Smith, "Quasars and Active Galaxies," in *The Universe,* ed. Byron Price (Toronto: Bantam Books, 1987), 192.
12. William J. Kaufmann, "The Black Hole," in *The Universe,* ed. Byron Price (Toronto: Bantam Books, 1987), 142.
13. K. C. Cole, "A Theory of Everything," *New York Times Magazine,* 18 October 1987, 22.
14. Cole, "A Theory of Everything," 28.
15. Tony Rothman, "The Seven Arrows of Time," *Discover,* February 1987, 62–77.
16. Rothman, "The Seven Arrows of Time," 66–67.
17. Stephen Hawking, *A Brief History of Time* (Toronto: Bantam Books, 1988), 133–53.
18. Rothman, "The Seven Arrows of Time," 77.
19. Shallis, *On Time,* 76.
20. Shallis, *On Time,* 79.
21. Shallis, *On Time,* 79, 81.
22. Alan Lightman, "Relativity for the Table," *Science 84,* 24. A number of authors have used the Doppler Effect to explain the redshift of light coming from distant galaxies. However, this phenomenon is more correctly interpreted as an "Expansion-red shift effect" resulting from the expansion of space, and not to the Doppler effect. See Edward R. Harrison, *Cosmology—The Science of the Universe* (Cambridge: Cambridge University Press, 1981), 237–40.
23. Lightman, "Relativity for the Table," 26.
24. Shallis, *On Time,* 56–57.
25. Sir John C. Eccles, *The Human Mystery* (London: Routledge and Kegan Paul, 1984), 10.
26. Sir John C. Eccles and Daniel N. Robinson, *The Wonder of Being Human,* (Boston: New Science Library, Shambhala, 1985), 27–28.

27. Eccles and Robinson, *The Wonder of Being Human,* 22–23.
28. Ibid., 25.
29. Ibid., 26.
30. Ibid.
31. Ibid., 35.
32. Ibid., 178.

10. God and the Future

We began this book with the idea that the God who has made this awesome and wonderful universe is utterly beyond our capacity to measure and yet is also the God who would be known. He has placed remarkable signs in the heavens, on Earth, and in ourselves: signals of transcendence. We conclude that this universe is here by divine plan, and that science itself, for decades a bastion of unbelief, has once again become the source for humankind's assurance of intimate divine concern in its affairs. We have looked at the origin of the universe and our own remarkable evolution, and found the whole punctuated with the supernatural. In Sir John Eccles's words,

We have the strong belief that we have to be open to the future in the adventure of human personhood. This whole cosmos is not just running on and running down for no meaning. In the context of natural theology we come to the belief that we are creatures with some supernatural meaning that is as yet ill defined. We cannot think more than that we are all part of some great design. Each of us can have the belief of acting in some unimaginable supernatural drama.[1]

Ralph Wendell Burhoe, in an article in *Zygon,* adds,

It is my view that the sciences add more than vital new evidence for the credibility of the essential wisdom of ancient theologies in recognizing the reality of a system of superhuman power that created, sustains, and selects us according to how well we meet its requirements for human life and advancement. The sciences also add far clearer evidence than we have had previously that the essential reality of evolving human life includes much more than our bodies: something as "inner" to us as our genes and innermost "feelings" and also something as lasting as "immortal souls."[2]

We have also observed the structure of the universe and concluded that it is pervaded with order and regularity, a theme repeated again and again even in the midst of seemingly chaotic events, as recently also observed by James Gleick in his book *Chaos*. [3] Finally, we have seen the thread of faith that runs through our entire 200,000-year history, and realized that we are inevitably religious creatures. Indeed, we have followed the light of the Light-giver in every age and in every culture. The conviction that comes is that even in our science we arrive at truth through faith— faith in an objective reality that lies beyond our empirical measurements and our theorizing. The rational order and structure of the universe that we observe derives not from some present idea or insight of ours, but from the rationality and faithfulness of the God who yet creates and sustains it. On our part there must be a commitment to receive this truth as we look away from ourselves to the objective source of truth, the Truth-giver. The power and fruitfulness of this approach has been the key to science's remarkable success. It is a program from which theology could greatly benefit, as we mentioned in Chapter 7 and as Walter Thorson discusses in more detail in his essay in Carl F. H. Henry's *Horizons of Science*. [4]

THE SCIENTIFIC FUTURE

The recent explosion in scientific knowledge has brought with it both euphoria and anxiety. Among scientists there have been those who have seen utopia almost within their grasp, and, indeed, it is exciting to anticipate such things as long-sought-after cures of traumatic illness, space exploration and colonization, and wonderful new philosophical insights. Among the last, we discussed in Chapter 6 the fascinating idea of implicate order as proposed by physicist David Bohm. Whereas Bohm applied the holographic paradigm to quantum physics, the idea has been applied in more recent years to a holographic view of the function of the human brain. One of the major contributors to the field is neurophysiologist Karl Pribram, who has found the holographic model to be especially attractive in explaining the enormous memory capacity of the human brain.[5] In a recent article in the magazine *Voice,* Michael Talbot tells us that the human brain is estimated to have the capacity to memorize about ten billion bits of information during the average human lifetime.[6] This is roughly the amount of information contained in five sets of the *Encyclopaedia Britannica.* But what is the mechanism for such information storage? Current theories rely on electrical fields or the flow of neurotransmitters, but none are very satisfying. Moreover, they are incapable of explaining the facility and sophistication of information retrieval, and they leave unexplained the nonselective nature of memory deficit. As far as memory is concerned, up to 20 percent of the brain may be surgically removed without affecting any memory component, and significantly greater removal leads only to a general haziness of memory, not selective loss.[7] The applicability of a holographic approach is almost obvious. As Pribram sees it, memories are encoded in patterns of nerve impulses that crisscross the brain in the same way that patterns of laser light interference crisscross the entire area of a film bearing a holographic image. This would explain how so much information is stored in so little space and how it can be retrieved so rapidly. Talbot comments,

Our uncanny ability to quickly retrieve whatever information we need from the enormous store of our memories becomes more understandable if the brain functions according to holographic principles. If a friends asks you to tell him what comes to mind when he says the word "zebra," you do not have to clumsily sort back through some gigantic and cerebral alphabetic file to arrive at an answer. Instead, associations like "striped," "horselike," and "animal native to Africa" all pop into your head instantly. Indeed, one of the most amazing things about the human thinking process is that every piece of information seems instantly cross-correlated with every other piece of information—another feature intrinsic to the hologram. Because every portion of a hologram is infinitely interconnected with every other portion, it is perhaps nature's supreme example of a cross-correlated system.[8]

But, in Talbot's view, the most striking implication of the holographic brain is seen when it is combined with Bohm's implicate order to yield a picture of the universe as a giant "superhologram," in which everything is connected to everything else as a maze of frequencies. In this view it is our brain's function to extract certain frequencies from this hologram and to mathematically transform them into sensory perceptions. Talbot sees this expression of the content of the universe in the form of a confused blur of frequencies as the loss of objective reality, but as we have seen, reality in the form of our models and mechanisms has a strange and elusive character. And, as we said earlier, our faith in the reality and rationality of the universe is a premise based upon our faith in the rationality of the God who creates and sustains it. Within that theological structure, the superhologram seems appropriate. Everything is connected to everything else by the immanent God, who holds the universe in being.

Perhaps the future will allow us to explore this realm of connectedness, possibly as a part of the sphere of the spirit, which first appeared with our Neandertal relatives. In a previous book one of us examined what the great religions have given as the "laws of the spirit," essential elements in the growth of the human spirit. Among these were a disciplined thought life, a generous and thankful spirit, a loving heart (which then becomes a channel for God's love), a forgiving attitude, and a willingness to surrender your life to a loving and all-powerful God. There it was pointed out that the laws of nature have been the subject of study for five centuries, but the scientific study of the laws of the spirit is in its infancy.[9] What is needed now is a program of research based upon new scientific methodologies to investigate and elaborate the patterns and laws governing spiritual growth and development. But this aspect of our being is far too important to be toyed with, especially in our own culture, where the "experimentation" often involves the use of extremely harmful drugs, and where exploitation and the profit motive are becoming major factors. Yet the goal of spiritual development is so extremely important to the realization of those ideals of integrity and generosity, compassion and humility, which are the noblest aspirations of our species. That goal is perhaps most succinctly stated by the prophet Micah near the close of the Old Testament: "He has showed you, O man, what is good: And what does the Lord require of you but to do justice, and to love kindness, and to walk humbly with your God."[10]

It is our impression that the description of the universe as a superhologram in purely scientific terms may be a gross speculation. Some behaviorists hope to explore and confirm the paranormal, and some scientists even speculate that we may someday simultaneously gain access to the past, present, and future, because all of history would be part of the giant hologram. But in contrast to these and other rather utopian possibilities for the future of science and spiritual values, there are more sober voices, which caution that the open-ended and speculative quality of present science and the success of technology have provoked a narrow preoccupation with the self. Rustum Roy challenges us, in his *Experimenting with Truth,* to be done with knowledge of any kind that is received for its own sake, without reference to action.[11] We are faced, in our culture, with an enormous preoccupation: with self, whether for the pursuit of our careers, or for the satisfaction of toying with new ideas, or exploring our inner selves. Paradoxically, this crisis of self-centeredness comes at just the point when you would expect, on the basis of our evolutionary journey, that we would be looking outward to others and upward to the Creator with the greatest expectation. The question Roy asks is, "How is this focus on self (this potential narcissism) to be tempered by concern for the other levels of society (community, nation, world) of which the same self is part?"[12] And, too, Roy asks a pointed question to those whose preoccupation may be theological: "How does all this square with at least the Christian, if not universal, religious tradition of self-denial, self-negation, at least of the postponement of gratification in the focus of concern for others?"[13] Jesus Christ's great admonition was, "If anyone would come after me, he must deny himself and take up his cross and follow me."[14]

As we said at the conclusion of Chapter 8, we have come a long way from the cave shelters of the Ice Age, but we believe, in God's great plan, we may have more to travel yet. Our science has brought us wondrous ideas and yet also some frightening prospects. With knowledge comes power, and in our day that power has taken on the awesome proportions of nuclear energy. For some it has been a means to grace, an opportunity to rethink old biases and old theologies. Loren Eiseley gives us an example in *The Firmament of Time:*

One of the chief architects of the atomic bomb, so the story runs, was out wandering in the woods one day with a friend when he came upon a small tortoise. Overcome with pleasurable excitement, he took up the tortoise and started home, thinking to surprise his children with it. After a few steps he paused and surveyed the tortoise doubtfully.

"What's the matter?" asked his friend.

Without responding, the great scientist slowly retraced his steps as precisely as possible, and gently set the turtle down upon the exact spot from which he had taken him up.

Then he turned solemnly to his friend. "It just struck me," he said, "that perhaps, for one man, I have tampered enough with the universe." He turned, and left the turtle to wander on its way.

The man who made that remark was one of the best of the modern men, and what he had devised had gone down into the whirlpool. "I have tampered enough," he said. It was not a denial of science. It was a final recognition that science is not enough for man. It is not the road back to the waiting Garden, for that road lies through the heart of man.[15]

But science has been enough to already reveal a Creation of awesome magnitude, intricacy, beauty, and order, and we sense that what lies beyond our instruments is vastly greater still. It is, finally, an experience that should bring us to our knees in humility, to worship the infinite, omniscient, eternal Creator.

Just a few months before his untimely death in 1944, William Temple, archbishop of Canterbury, broadcasting over the BBC, made the statement,

The world will be saved from political chaos and collapse by one thing only: That is worship.

Then he gave a definition of worship:

To quicken the conscience by the holiness of God,
To feed the mind with the truth of God,

To purge the imagination with the beauty of God,
To open the heart to the love of God,
To devote the will to the purpose of God.[16]

NOTES

1. Sir John C. Eccles and Daniel N. Robinson, *The Wonder of Being Human* (Boston: New Science Library, Shambhala, 1985), 178–79.
2. Ralph Wendell Burhoe, "The Human Prospect and the Lord of History," *Zygon: Journal of Religion and Science* 10 (1975): 299.
3. James Gleick, *Chaos: Making a New Science* (New York: Viking, 1987), 152, 172, 219, 304–17.
4. Walter R. Thorson, "The Spiritual Dimensions of Science," in *Horizons of Science: Christian Scholars Speak Out,* ed. Carl F. H. Henry (San Francisco: Harper & Row, 1977), 217–57.
5. John P. Briggs and F. David Peat, *Looking Glass Universe* (New York: Cornerstone Library, Simon & Schuster, 1984), 236–68.
6. Michael Talbot, "The Universe as Hologram," *Voice,* 22 Sept. 1987, 31.
7. Briggs and Peat, *Looking Glass Universe,* 242.
8. Talbot, "The Universe as Hologram," 31.
9. John M. Templeton, *The Humble Approach* (New York: Seabury Press, 1981), 118–28.
10. Micah 6:8, RSV.
11. Rustum Roy, *Experimenting with Truth* (Oxford: Pergamon Press, 1981), 180, 189–90.
12. Roy, *Experimenting with Truth,* 189.
13. Roy. *Experimenting with Truth,* 190.
14. Mark 8:34, NIV.
15. Loren Eiseley, *The Firmament of Time* (New York: Atheneum, 1984), 148–49.
16. William Temple, "The Hope of a New World", *The Search for God,* ed. David M. White (New York: Macmillan, 1983), 151.

Acknowledgments

The following publishers have generously given permission for the use of quotations from copyrighted works: From *The Way the World Is,* by John Polkinghorne. Copyright 1983. Reprinted by permission of Triangle/SPCK, London. From *Experimenting with Truth,* by Rustum Roy. Copyright 1981 by the Hibbert Trust. Reprinted by permission of Pergamon Press. From *The Universe and Dr. Einstein,* by Lincoln Barnett. Copyright 1948 by Harper & Brothers, 1950 and 1957 by Lincoln Barnett. Reprinted by permission of William Morrow and Company. From *Creation and the World of Science,* by Arthur Peacocke. Copyright 1979. Reprinted by permission of Oxford University Press. From *Divine and Contingent Order,* by Thomas F. Torrance, Oxford University Press. Copyright 1981. Reprinted by permission of the author. From *The Clockwork Image,* by Donald M. MacKay. Copyright 1974 by InterVarsity Press, London. Reprinted by permission of Dr. Valerie MacKay. From "Aurora Leigh," by Elizabeth Barrett Browning in *The Complete Poetical Works of Elizabeth Barrett Browning, Book VII.* Copyright 1900 by Houghton Mifflin Company. Reprinted by permission. From "A Scientist's Psalm," by Walter R. Hearn. Copyright 1963. Reprinted by *HIS* magazine, InterVarsity Press, Downers Grove, IL. Reprinted by permission of the author. From "Modern Cosmogony & Biblical Creation," edited by Roland Frye in *Is God A Creationist.* Copyright 1983 by Owen Gingerich and Charles Scribner and Sons. Reprinted by permission of the author. From "The Promise of Structuralist Ethics," by Gunther Stent in *The Hastings Center Report, No. 6.* Reprinted by permission of The Hastings Center Briarcliff Manor, New York and Gunther Stent. From "To the Dizzy Edge," by Alan Lightman in *Science 82,* October 1982, (also in *Time Travel and Papa Joe's Pipe*). Copyright 1982 by the AAAS. Reprinted by permission of the author. From "Relativity for the Table," by Alan Lightman in *Science 84,* 1984, (also in *Time Travel and Papa Joe's Pipe*). Copyright 1984 by the AAAS. Reprinted by permission of the author. From "The Scientific Aesthetic," by K. C. Cole in *Discover,* December 1983. Copyright 1983 by K. C. Cole and Discover Publications. Reprinted by permission. From "The Seven Arrows of Time," by Tony Rothman in *Discover,* February 1987. Copyright 1987 by Tony Rothman and Discover Publications. Reprinted by permission. From *The Christian Frame of Mind,* by Thomas F. Torrance. Copyright 1985 by The Handsel Press. Reprinted by permission. From "Science and the Sense of Self," by Lynn White, Jr. in *Limits of Scientific Inquiry,* edited by Holton & Morrison. Copyright 1979. Reprinted by permission of Norton. From *Order Out of Chaos,* by Ilya Prigogine and Isabelle Stengers. Copyright 1984 by Ilya Prigogine and Isabelle Stengers. Reprinted by permission of Bantam Books, a division of Bantam, Doubleday, Dell Publishing Group, Inc. From *Grammatical Man,* by Jeremy Campbell. Copyright 1982 by Jeremy Campbell. Reprinted by permission of Simon & Schuster. From *Looking Glass Universe,* by John Briggs and F. David Peat. Copyright 1984 by John Briggs and F. David Peat. Reprinted by permission of Simon & Schuster. From *Mere Christianity,* by C. S. Lewis. Copyright 1943, 1945, 1952 by Macmillan and by C. S. Lewis. Reprinted by permission of William Collins, Sons & Co., London. From "The Hope of a New World," by William Temple in *The Search for God,* by David M. White. Copyright 1983 by David M. White. Reprinted by permission of Macmillan. From "All Things are Full of God," by John S. Blackie in *The Search for God,* by David M. White. Copyright 1983 by David M. White. Reprinted by permission of Macmillan. From *A Rumor of Angels,* by Peter Berger. Copyright 1969 by Peter Berger. Reprinted by permission of Doubleday, a division of Bantam, Doubleday, Dell Publishing Group, Inc. From *The Firmament of Time,* by Loren Eiseley. Copyright 1960 by Loren Eiseley and the Trustees of the University of Pennsylvania. Reprinted with the permission of Atheneum Publishers, an imprint of Macmillan. From the poem "Ode to a Pet Chimpanzee," by Arden Almquist in *The Covenant Companion.* Copyright 1985 by Arden Almquist. Reprinted by permission of Covenant Publishers, Chicago, IL. From *The Unexpected Universe,* by Loren Eiseley. Copyright 1969 by Loren Eiseley. Reprinted by permission of Harcourt Brace Jovanovich. From *On Time,* by Michael Shallis. Copyright 1982 by Michael Shallis. Reprinted by permission of Schocken Books, New York. From the *Journal of the American Scientific Affiliation* or *Perspectives on Science and Christian Faith.* Reprinted by permission. From *The Road of Science and the Ways to God,* by Stanley L. Jaki. Copyright 1978 by the University of Chicago. Reprinted by permission. From "On Taking Vows in Two Priesthoods," by Robert L. Herrmann in *Yale Journal of Biology and Medicine.* Copyright 1976 by Academic Press. Reprinted by permission of Academic Press.

Index

80433

LINCOLN CHRISTIAN COLLEGE AND SEMINARY

261.55
T288